THE DARWIN AWARDS
COUNTDOWN TO EXTINCTION

WENDY NORTHCUTT is a scientist and graduate of UC Berkeley with a degree in molecular biology. She began collecting the stories that make up the Darwin Awards in 1993 and founded www.Darwin Awards.com soon thereafter. She lives in San Jose, California.

Praise for *The Darwin Awards*

"Delightfully funny . . . If you are not yet aware of *The Darwin Awards*, you should probably be pitched out of the breeding population . . . taken together they constitute a delicious sermon in support of common sense."   —*The Baltimore Sun*

"A warning to all dimwits."   —Salon.com

"Hilarious . . . Books are often defined as good by saying you can't put it down. With *Darwin Awards* you can. Then pick it up again. And again."   —*The Flint Journal* (Michigan)

"One of the drawbacks to not teaching the theory of evolution in schools is that some people wind up learning stuff the hard way. . . . One lesson is that fatal stupidity knows no boundaries."   —*Sarasota Herald-Tribune*

"A riot to read. Deeply entertaining."   —*San Francisco Weekly*

the
darwin Āwards ®

COUNTDOWN
TO EXTINCTION

WENDY NORTHCUTT

A PLUME BOOK

The Darwin Awards Countdown to Extinction contains cautionary tales of misadventure. It is intended to be a safety manual, not a how-to guide. The stories illustrate evolution working through natural selection. Those whose actions have lethal personal consequences are ushered out of the gene pool. Your decisions can kill you, so pay attention and stay alive.

PLUME
Published by the Penguin Group
Penguin Group (USA) Inc., 375 Hudson Street, New York, New York 10014, U.S.A.; Penguin Group (Canada), 90 Eglinton Avenue East, Suite 700, Toronto, Ontario, Canada M4P 2Y3 (a division of Pearson Penguin Canada Inc.); Penguin Books Ltd., 80 Strand, London WC2R 0RL, England; Penguin Ireland, 25 St. Stephen's Green, Dublin 2, Ireland (a division of Penguin Books Ltd.); Penguin Group (Australia), 250 Camberwell Road, Camberwell, Victoria 3124, Australia (a division of Pearson Australia Group Pty. Ltd.); Penguin Books India Pvt. Ltd., 11 Community Centre, Panchsheel Park, New Delhi – 110 017, India; Penguin Group (NZ), 67 Apollo Drive, Rosedale, Auckland 0632, New Zealand (a division of Pearson New Zealand Ltd.); Penguin Books (South Africa) (Pty.) Ltd., 24 Sturdee Avenue, Rosebank, Johannesburg 2196, South Africa

Penguin Books Ltd., Registered Offices: 80 Strand, London WC2R 0RL, England

Published by Plume, a member of Penguin Group (USA) Inc. Previously published in a Dutton edition.

First Plume Printing, November 2011
10 9 8

Illustrations by Kevin Buckley
DARWIN AWARDS® is registered in the U.S. Patent and Trademark Office.

Ⓟ REGISTERED TRADEMARK—MARCA REGISTRADA

The Library of Congress has catalogued the Dutton edition as follows:
Northcutt, Wendy.
The Darwin Awards countdown to extinction / Wendy Northcutt.
p. cm.
ISBN 978-0-525-95191-9 (hc.)
ISBN 978-0-452-29736-4 (pbk.)
1. Stupidity—Anecdotes.   2. Stupidity—Humor.   I. Title.
BF431.N676   2010
081—dc22   2010033039

Printed in the United States of America
Original hardcover design by Daniel Lagin

Dedicated to helpful, loving people:

Kevin Buckley quit his job to illustrate this book!

Many a pleasant evening has been spent discussing death with the likes of Eric Biederman, Alicia *&* Brian Nitpick Watrous, Peter and Suzi Anvin, Kathleen and Brian De Smet, Tara Tolles, Lisa Davis, Krista Anderson, and many other patient, witty people. Ariane La Gauche sprinkled enchanting turns of phrase everywhere. Stephen Darksyde edited science essays—free! And generous volunteer moderators continue to make the whole system work.

Thank you, Tommy Kay Levin, for much more than feeding me. Thank you, Joe da Rosa of Bodyworks Specialists, for making house calls.

and . . .

Thank you, Greg Levin, for fetching coffee in the morning.

Thank you for washing laundry and being a quiet kitchen elf.

Thank you for editing essays with me during long car drives.

Thanks for reassembling the drawer that fell apart over that *godforsaken oubliette*.

Thank you for playing Race for the Galaxy *whenever* and *wherever* I want.

Thank you for finding my cell phone.

Thank you for finding my purse too.

Thank you for finding *me*.

Nine no-no's with power tools
Eight ways to incinerate yourself
Seven safety warnings not to ignore
Six sexy survival tips
Five fiery fiascos
Four Double Darwins
Three watery whoops!
Two damaged digits
One delightful book of doom
Now, with zombies!

CONTENTS

What do the families think?
I have kids. Am I safe?
Are humans really evolving?
Isn't there something beautiful about moronic creativity?
Why so many men?
Why do we laugh at death?
What inspired you to do this?
What are your aspirations?
How many stories? How many books? How many more?
Are you making a movie, musical, or TV show?
Do you drive while using a cell phone?
What were those Five (5) Rules, again?

the darwinAwards®

COUNTDOWN TO EXTINCTION

INTRODUCTION

The Darwin Awards, named in honor of Charles Darwin, salute the improvement of the human genome by commemorating those who accidentally remove themselves from it—thereby ensuring that the next generation is descended from one less idiot. Of necessity, this honor is usually bestowed posthumously.

To win a Darwin Award, an adult must eliminate himself from the gene pool in an astonishingly stupid way that is verifiably true. Most stories are verified by news reports or by reliable eyewitnesses such as emergency responders.

Past winners include a thief who thought it was wise to steal copper wire without shutting off the electric current, and a farmer who avoided bee stings by sealing his head in a plastic bag. We have also honored individuals who offered a bear a beer, jumped a drawbridge gap on a motorbike, or peered into a gas tanker with a lighter.

This book is packed with a pirate's booty of new winners and at-risk survivors. We begin with the following surprise nominee . . .

At-Risk Survivor: Meet the Author!
"Breaking" News

AUGUST 2009, CALIFORNIA | Wendy "Darwin" Northcutt, writer of humorous obituaries and author of six Darwin Awards books, nearly made her own dark list in a clever attempt to cool her house. During a California heat wave, she opened up a grate in the hallway floor intending to install a fan and, by this device, force basement air up into the house. Before she could finish the air-conditioning job, the phone rang.

Distracted, three hours passed before Wendy wandered back down the hall and fell through the grate. The author nearly became the eponymous Darwin Award winner. Thankfully this time she survived, and a broken leg was the price she paid for the lesson: *Never walk away from a hole in the floor.*

Reader Comments

"I'd recommend walking away from holes. It's turning around and *walking back* that's dangerous."

"If you can walk away from such an experience—be 'grate'ful!"

". . . and she *works* for Mr. Darwin!"

Now, let's dive into a sea of stories about those who flounder in the shallow end of the gene pool!

CHAPTER 11

FOOD: OUT TO LUNCH!

"I don't believe in evolution, but sometimes you realize that it *would* be beneficial to the human race!"

—Fan mail

In the mood for a sweet treat? Humans nourish themselves on high-voltage cake batter, fruitcake firebombs, and chewing gum that will blow your mind. In the mood to *be* a treat? Read on for encounters with submerged crocodiles, decidedly un-docile deer, lethal ligers, and zombies! These people are literally *out to lunch*.

*Doublemint Dumb Chewing Gum • Not Fast Enough Food •
Teeming with Crocodiles • Ninja Deer Hunter • The Mane
Attraction • Not Even Half-Baked • The Great Fruitcake Incident
• Hot Buns • Hard Science, with Zombies!*

Darwin Award Winner:
Doublemint Dumb Chewing Gum

Confirmed by Darwin

Featuring food, explosions, and science!

5 DECEMBER 2009, RUSSIA | A twenty-five-year-old chemistry student of the Kiev Polytechnic Institute had the peculiar habit of dipping his chewing gum in citric acid crystals while he worked, presumably to add a tart, zesty flavor. He was hunched over at a computer in his parents' house in the city of Konotop when, whether by intention or inattention, the student dunked his gum into an unidentified chemical explosive and stuck it back into his mouth.

According to news reports, "a loud pop" was heard coming from his room.

Putting aside the question of why he was doing chemistry at home, the student was well aware of the need to keep chemicals away from food. Every laboratory emphasizes the importance of "No Food!" because it is easy to drink the wrong liquid or salt your salad with arsenic. He knew better. But there he was, deceased, the lower part of his face blown off.

A forensic examination established that the remains of the chewing gum was covered with a dangerous substance that the

local laboratory did not have the necessary equipment to identify. Police found packets of citric acid and packets of a similar-looking explosive material, and think the student simply confused the two.

Reference: lenta.ru, en.rian.ru, RIA Novosti

Reader Comments

"The new chewing gum that will blow your mind!"

"Must have been one heckuva of a bubble."

"The ultimate bubble!"

"The flavor blew him away."

"This is a jaw dropper."

"He really lost his head."

Darwin Award Winner: Not Fast Enough Food

Confirmed by Darwin
Featuring food and a liger!

30 OCTOBER 2008, OKLAHOMA | Peter G., thirty-two, was an accomplished big cat keeper. With his huge heart and ability to connect with animals, this former Tulsa Zookeeper was the perfect volunteer at Safari's Animal Sanctuary in Broken Arrow. Perfect—until the Liger Incident.

You may ask, as we asked, "What's a liger?"

Ligers are unusual animals, a sterile cross between a male lion and a female tiger, and (like mules) not a species in their own right. Although a liger is an evolutionary dead end, this powerful hybrid is the largest of big cats. Rocky, the liger that lived in Broken Arrow, was considered to be a big baby—yet he was not, by any means, a domestic animal. The wildlife sanctuary manager said, "In all my years we've stressed that whatever you do, *don't* open that gate."

"Peter did not follow very obvious safety rules."

Peter opened that gate.

For reasons unknown, he entered the liger cage during feeding time, only to become an appetizer for the hungry carnivore. Although he dragged himself out of the cage before becoming the main course, he died in the hospital that night.

Peter was loved, and he will be missed. But he was

well aware of the dangers posed by captive wild animals. By not following very obvious safety rules, Peter was behaving with all the care and caution typical of a Darwin Award winner.

Burp.

Reference: *Daily Mail*, dailymail.co.uk, cryptomundo.com

Reader Comments

"Fancy Feast."

"Human-meat kitty treat."

A **liger** is a hybrid cross between a male lion (*Panthera leo*) and a female tiger (*Panthera tigris*). A **tiglon** is a hybrid cross between a male tiger and a female lion. Ligers and tiglons exist only in captivity because the parent species' territories do not overlap. Ligers typically grow to enormous sizes while tiglons do not exceed the size of either parent. Male ligers and tiglons are sterile but females occasionally produce offspring. Tiglon-lion cubs are known as litigons, and tiglon-tiger cubs are called titigons!

Darwin Award Winner:
Teeming with Crocodiles

Confirmed by Darwin

Featuring a woman, water, food, and a crocodile

1 JANUARY 2010, SOUTH AFRICA | Pop quiz, class! Do you or don't you go swimming in the crocodile-infested Limpopo River? Do you or don't you leave your friends on the banks of the great gray-green Limpopo and swim in its dark and ominous waters? Let's just say it was a short New Year for Mariska B., twenty-seven, a waitress and former swimmer.

According to a long-time resident of Phalaborwa, locals know, "You don't even put a toe in the river. It's teeming with crocodiles and hippos." But Mariska—a local who knew better—went into the waters of the Olifants River (the main tributary to the Limpopo) not once, not twice, but three times that day. And on her third refreshing dip of the day, she didn't have time to scream or struggle; friends saw just a ripple on the water where seconds before she **Olifants = Elephants** had been swimming. Swimming, metaphorically, in the shallow end.

Did I mention that the river was strictly prohibited? Police searched for Mariska's body with long poles, and with the sensi-

tive chemical detectors known as sniffer dogs, but found no trace. The cycle of life continues.

Reference: News24.com

Reader Comment

"The world is not a petting zoo."

"If the police had sent in divers looking for the body,
serial Darwin Awards could have been issued.
Happily, justice was blind but not stupid."

At-Risk Survivor: Ninja Deer Hunter

Unconfirmed Personal Account

Featuring hunting, food, and a deer

1996, TEXAS | My father's friend, Joe, was out in one of the many hunting leases in southeast Texas, looking for a delicious hunk of venison on the hoof. When he failed to return to home base, his worried wife went to check on him. She found him in an unconscious state with blood and puncture wounds all about his body! Joe suffered no lasting damage, despite his incredibly risky misadventure:

That morning he had been in a climbing stand up in a tree above an open creek bottom—his favorite spot—when he heard a deer blow at his back. He didn't risk turning to look, for fear of spooking the animal, so he quietly waited . . . until a large buck sauntered just under the tree he was in! Apparently he did not have time to carefully determine his best course of action. Rather than lean down and shoot the animal in the head, an easy kill, he opted to attack with a large hunting knife.

Positioning himself in a catlike crouch, he pounced on the deer, intending to close the deal on what could have been an awesome deer-slaying story. But when he landed, the trajectory of the knife was slightly askew. He swung the blade under the buck's throat and into his own opposing thigh.

Since he landed on the animal's neck, it had no trouble determining its *own* best course of action. It threw its large rack back into the man's face. Follow-

He did not have time to carefully determine his best course of action.

ing the head butt the hunter lost consciousness, and what followed is clear speculation based on the blood trail and shreds of clothing. He appeared to have been dragged about forty yards across the forest floor before his flannel jacket—being the main reason for staying on the buck after the eight-second buzzer—tore loose and released him from the beast.

In time, he healed completely, and that stand is still Joe's favorite hunting spot!

Reference: Grady Woods

Deer occasionally gain an advantage over their primary predators. "I had this idea that I was going to catch a deer, put it in a stall, sweet feed it on corn for a few weeks, then butcher it. Yum! Corn-fed venison. The first step in this adventure was acquiring a live deer. . . ." Things go from bad to worse in "Roping a Deer," from *Darwin Awards Next Evolution: Chlorinating the Gene Pool* (Plume, 2009).

Read more: www.DarwinAwards.com/book/deer

At-Risk Survivor: The Mane Attraction

Unconfirmed

Featuring food, a lion, the military, and insurance

2009, POLAND | One day a young man living in Wroclaw received a large envelope in the mail. One look and he knew exactly what it was: the draft. In Poland, when a man turns eighteen he is summoned to the medical commission to determine whether he is healthy enough to serve his country.

There are ways to avoid being conscripted. For instance, being enrolled in higher education or providing sole financial support for a child or suffering a serious physical handicap. Our boy was completely healthy, had no kids, and was not smart enough to continue his education. In short, he was destined to serve his country. And he was determined to avoid it.

The Polish medical commission has four categories:

A. In good health, and able to serve in the army.
D. Able to serve only during wartime.
E. Completely unable to serve, even during war.
B. Temporarily unable to pass the medical exam; e.g., recovering from an accident but expected to return to full health. "B" candidates must attend another medical commission in twelve months.

Our hero wanted Category B, and another twelve months to find some way of cheating the army. But

The big cat decided that such insolence must be punished.

how? While playing with his cat, he was accidentally scratched, and *bang*! The idea was formed. A few serious scratches and stitches would qualify him for a deferment.

Our man decided that a small cat was not enough, which leads us to the Wroclaw zoo. The incidental spectators watched in amazement as he strode toward the lion cage, reached inside, and started yelling at a large male beast. The King of Cats looked in amusement upon the small being stubbornly trying to provoke him, but when the little hominid pulled its handsome mane, the big cat decided that such insolence must be punished.

Our man's plan worked better than he expected. He received not a B, but an E. You see, the irate lion did not simply scratch the idiot. It used its powerful jaws to bite the man's arm off.

This story was aired on Polish TV when the amputee sued his insurance company for failure to pay for the missing arm. The company successfully asserted that it does not cover the loss of a limb due to the bite of an intentionally provoked lion.

Reference: Polish TV

Reader Comment

"A piece of advice: *Never* avoid the draft by provoking a lion."

At-Risk Survivor: Not Even Half-Baked

Unconfirmed Personal Account

Featuring food, a woman, and electricity

Fewer and more fastidious, female Darwin Award contenders prefer more wholesome methods for their special acts.

After an extended night shift, our heroine, a working mother, was exhausted but decided to stay up a few extra hours until the kids came home from school. Being a thoughtful mom and a junk-food junkie, the tired woman decided that this was the time to bake a cake.

Her ancient yellow electric mixer had a detachable cord that plugged into the back of the appliance. Things were going well—butter, sugar, flour, cocoa—until the loose cord popped out of the old mixer and landed in the dough. *Plop.*

Ever the safety-conscious professional, she carefully turned off and set aside the completely inert mixer, and lifted the cord out of the batter. But what did she do with cake batter dripping off the end of the cord? She did what anyone would do—she stuck the live electrical cord in her mouth and found herself on the floor, suddenly very wide awake. Did I mention that the old cord was ungrounded?

Having lived to tell the tale *and* having reproduced, she is twice disqualified from winning the Darwin Award, but there is an ironic twist. Who would relate such an idiotic thing? Who would be dumb enough to electrify herself mouth first, and honest enough to use it as a safety lesson afterward? Only an Occupational First Aid instructor, introducing the learning module on electric shock!

What happened to the cake is anyone's guess.

Reference: A student of the First Aid Instructor

WENDY'S DEADLY DINNER PARTY

To celebrate the publication of a new Darwin Awards book, the author hosted a dinner party featuring Suspicious Mushroom Soup, E. Coli Spinach Salad, Faux Fugu, and assorted deadly delectable and toxic treats. Her centerpriece was carefully picked branch of poison oak, carried home from a walk wrapped in layers of fabric, and carefully transferred to a high-walled glass display vessel. Three days latter . . . your guessed it: She developed a pernicious poison oak rash. The moral of the story is, there is *no such thing as picking poison oak safely*.

"He who teaches himself has a fool for a master."
—Benjamin Franklin

At-Risk Survivor:
The Great Fruitcake Incident

Confirmed Personal Account

Featuring a father, food, holidays, an explosion, and alcohol

A holiday-themed personal account, with one more reason to be leery of too much Christmas cheer.

2005 | I love cooking. Every year I bake a few fruitcakes for family and neighbors. I mix in various alcohols, so people actually *eat* my fruitcakes. Now, I've been known to experiment with various types of alcohol. In 2005, I was suffering from a shortage of Jack Daniel's whiskey, so I searched the kitchen and settled on a bottle of tequila. After mixing a measure of the Mexican liquor into the batter, I poured it and slid the pan home.

> **I was suffering from a shortage of Jack Daniel's whiskey.**

Alcohol burns, so when you bake a fruitcake you use a low temperature. Set the oven no higher than 250 degrees so your cakes don't catch on fire—never a good thing, and besides, it's hard to explain why the top of the cake is charred.

As I slid the pan in, my father came into the room. He also loved cooking, and he was darn good at it. Poking around, he started making suggestions. I remember seeing him look at my oven, look back at me, and laugh. "You'll never get it done like *that*." He reached over and turned the heat up to 350°F.

I stood there dazed, the smell of fruitcake and burnt hair filling the air.

Remembering my previous flambé, I sighed and reached toward the stove. I started to say, "Dad, you have to cook it that low, alcohol . . ." But all I had uttered was, "Dad . . ." when my hand touched the knob. There was this loud *WHOMP*! The oven door blew open and a sheet of blue flame shot straight up out of it, burning *all* the hair off my arm—which never grew back!

I stood there dazed, the smell of fruitcake and burnt hair filling the air, my dad with a look of utter shock on his face. Before heading to the ER, which he was nice enough to take me to, I managed to finish my sentence: "Alcohol burns."

And *you* try explaining to the ER that your fruitcake exploded . . .

Reference: Chad Peters, in loving memory of his father, Harold Peters

Reader Comments

"More than one fruitcake in that kitchen."

"Now we know why fruitcake is lucky."

A concerned reader pointed out: "This doesn't fill the bill, since the independent actions of two people who didn't communicate fast enough were not, taken separately, stupid acts on the part of either." The reader is correct. Since no self-selection is evident in The Great Fruitcake Incident, the son would *not* earn a Darwin Award if things had turned out badly.

At-Risk Survivor: Hot Buns

Confirmed by Darwin
Featuring food, work, and an oven

FEBRUARY 2009, SWEDEN | Welcome to Sweden, home of Swedish massage, Swedish fish, and one Swedish meatball who decided to warm himself in an industrial-strength oven. The incident took place during a freezing February at a facility operated by a maker of kitchen cabinets and fixtures.

The heating system in the loading area had ceased to function, leaving a shivering truck driver defenseless against the frigid winter. Looking to escape the cold, this driver wandered toward the large oven used for shrink-wrapping and asked the operator if he could take a spin on the oven's conveyor belt to get warm! Although the driver was freezing his umlaut off, the hard-hearted operator denied the man's request.

Undaunted, the driver waited until no one was looking . . .

Undaunted, the driver waited until no one was looking and managed to hoist himself onto the conveyor belt for a blissful, toasty ride. But all those Swedish smorgasbords had taken their toll. The massive trucker was too heavy for the belt and the motor shut down, leaving him stuck in the 180°C (360°F) oven!

Luckily the oven operator noticed the stoppage and was able to rescue the man from the searing heat before he sustained serious damage. Following the incident, Sweden's Work Environment Authority offered the oven operator counseling to work through the shock he suffered and intends to carry out a risk assessment of surveillance around the shrink-wrap ovens. Apparently they are too tempting to leave unguarded.

Reference: Fox News, thelocal.se

Reader Comments

"Talk about a hot and cold personality!"
"Hot stuff."
"Hot lips!"

For the scientific or artistic mind, a shrink-wrap oven offers fascinating possibilities. The unfortunate masses who do not own an expensive shrink-wrap oven can use household appliances such as a hair dryer to good effect. For those with sufficient courage and an oven broiler, an empty potato chip bag can be reduced to the size of a postage stamp—with the words *still legible* in miniature! An intriguing glimpse into the world of home shrink-wrap experimentation:

How to Shrink a Bag of Chips
www.DarwinAwards.com/book/shrinkchips

At-Risk Survivor:
Hard Science, with Zombies!

Unconfirmed Personal Account
Featuring food and a hammer

2010 | Ray and I are great fans of zombie movies and have passed many a late night in front of the TV with popcorn and DVDs. Ever since reading the *Zombie Survival Guide* by Max Brooks, Ray is convinced that hordes of the undead will one day rise up. While trying to convince me of the impending apocalypse, Ray cited two facts that I found to be in error.

1. The human skull is one of the hardest surfaces in nature.
2. A medieval mace lacks the stopping power to crush it.

We argued these points for half an hour, without coming to an agreement.

The next morning Ray texted me to come over and settle the issue. He answered the door wearing a cycle helmet and led me to the backyard, where he handed me a lump hammer (a small sledge) and told me to hit him over the head. I don't know if the helmet would have stopped the hammer blow or not, and I wasn't about to try it on my friend. Instead I devised a simple experiment, hoping to avoid any nasty injuries.

Ray and I went to the supermarket to buy two coconuts, one for the experiment and one because I really like coconut. We returned to the backyard and

SILLY SCIENCE

Zombies eat people. But do zombies eat dead people? According to Matt Mogk at the Zombie Research Society, the answer is important. If zombies continue feeding after their victims are dead, then they are effectively destroying their own reinforcements. That would be a Darwinian move.

proceeded to place a coconut on the paving. I picked up the lump hammer and with one solid blow, reduced the coconut to delicious shrapnel. As I was clearing up the shards of nutty goodness, I said, "If that was your head, you'd be dead."

I turned to see Ray trying to validate my theory—by head butting the second coconut as hard as he could! Ray was fine after a few stitches, thankfully not a Darwin Award winner this time, but I'll keep you posted.

Incidentally Ray was vindicated. He did manage to crack the nut with a head butt. Since he proved that his skull is indeed harder than a coconut, my experiment was inconclusive.

Reference: Pete Copping

Reader Comments

"The unbearable hardness of being."

"Jesus was a Zombie!"

SCIENCE INTERLUDE
THE MYSTERY OF SUPER-TOXIC
SNAKE VENOM

By Michael Wall

*(who managed to write this whole essay without
using the word* snakebite *even once!)*

Too Much of a Nasty Thing?

On March 4, 2008, a juvenile black mamba bit Nathan Layton as
he hiked in the bush west of South Africa's Kruger National Park.
The twenty-eight-year-old Englishman was training to be a game
ranger and was in good shape, yet he sank into a coma almost immediately and died within an hour. Layton is not under consideration for a Darwin Award—he was just unlucky enough to get nailed
by one of the world's most dangerous snakes.

Black mambas are fast, agile, nervous, and big, reaching lengths
up to fourteen feet. Among venomous snakes, only the king
cobra grows longer. Mambas and cobras, their hooded
cousins, belong to the family Elapidae and share a po-
tent neurotoxic venom. Its effects are dramatic. A
victim's neurons no longer transmit messages, mus-

Kill Bill, a macabre comedy film, features assassins named after deadly snakes: Black Mamba, Cottonmouth, Copperhead, and Sidewinder. Two thumbs-up for Tarantino's powerful ode to motherhood.

cles fail to respond to the simplest command, and bitten animals asphyxiate as the venom scrambles nerve signals that tell the diaphragm to expand and contract.

As Layton's quick death indicates, black mamba venom is powerful: The venom from a single bite can kill 9,400 lab mice. But mambas aren't the toxicity champs, not by a long shot; at least twenty-two other snakes pack more of a wallop. At the top of the list is Australia's inland taipan. This shy, inoffensive serpent—which the late Steve Irwin let tongue-flick his cheek on one episode of *The Crocodile Hunter*—can snuff out 100,000 lab mice with the venom from a single bite.

These toxins are much more powerful than snakes seem to need. It's like they're rabbit hunting with a bazooka. And the mystery deepens when you consider how costly venom is to produce. One study showed that after being "milked," rattlesnakes and other pit vipers jack up their metabolic rate by 11 percent for at least three days to refill their glands. So shouldn't natural selection discourage snakes from making excessively toxic venom?

It should, and it does. Snakes aren't as loose with their venom as we may think.

Mamba venom did not evolve to kill humans or lab mice. Prey animals are tough, so snakes count on their venom to immobilize their prey, and to do so *fast*. Many venomous snakes tackle feisty, sharp-toothed prey that can outweigh them by 50 percent—

Venomous Dinosaurs? A recent fossil analysis provides the most detailed evidence yet that some dinosaurs hunted with venom. Sinornithosaurus, a carnivorous Chinese dinosaur that lived 65–100 million years ago, had fanglike front teeth and a large bony pocket in its upper jaw that likely contained a venom gland. In modern venomous taxa, this type of fang discharges venom along a groove on the outer surface of the tooth.

formidable foes, especially for animals without arms or legs. A single bite from a wood rat, for example, can snip right through a western diamondback rattlesnake's spine.

The hypertoxicity of a rattlesnake's venom helps it prevent this personal tragedy by knocking the rat out in a matter of seconds. The rattlesnake does not care whether his bite *could* dispatch a hundred lab mice, or a thousand. All that matters is that it dispatches one rat with a minimum of muss and fuss before the rat has a chance to dispatch him. Super-toxic venom can thus be thought of as a defensive adaptation: It helps keep snakes safe from prey.

The threat of prey retaliation has been important in snake evolution. For example, many venomous species—including rattlesnakes—instinctively strike and release rodents, then hang back and wait for the reeling animal to keel over. Powerful venom prevents dinner from staggering too far off. By contrast, smaller, less dangerous prey such as lizards are often simply choked down, still struggling.

Extreme toxicity can do more than knock prey

out. For example, it can—and often does—help snakes digest their dinners. This is a big deal to serpents, which swallow large animals whole.

Think about that western diamondback again. It strikes a wood rat, tracks the dying animal by homing in on the scent of its own venom, and swallows the prey in one long gulp. Snakes don't chew their food, so now the snake has an intact rodent clogging its gut.

Such a meal, tempting as it is, would rot inside us before we had a chance to process it. The rattlesnake, however, has an edge: Its venom is packed with proteins that break down tissue. The snake starts digesting the rat from the inside out the moment its inch-long fangs penetrate the rodent's furry flesh. Tissue-dissolving venom is a key adaptation that allows rattlesnakes and other vipers to consume absurdly large prey.

> The bite of a juvenile snake, as most hikers know, can be more dangerous than the bite of an adult. Young snakes are more nervous and have not yet learned to conserve ammunition!

Another reason snake venoms are so toxic is that prey animals are tough. Animals often evolve a degree of resistance to their predators. California ground squirrels, for example, have proteins in their blood that blunt the effects of rattlesnake venom. Sure, a black mamba bite can snuff 9,400 lab mice. But a true assessment of mamba venom toxicity would measure its power to kill natural prey such as African rats. These experiments are seldom done, for it is far easier to work with common, inbred lab mice. But it's a sure bet that venom from one mamba bite cannot take out 9,400 wild African rats.

Hunter and hunted are engaged in a chemical arms race and have been for millions of years. Lab mice, and the unfortunate Nathan Layton, never joined this race and are pretty much defenseless. Using them to gauge the strength of mamba venom is like testing a Tomahawk missile against a leather shield. The real-world potency of venom is likely far less than our inflated, artificial estimates.

So give snakes a break. Only about 10 percent of the world's three thousand snake species are venomous enough to be dangerous to man, and they're dangerous for good reason: They're as nasty as natural selection dictates they should be. Yet they're merciful, too. Remember the poor wood rat that became a meal for our western diamondback? He was unconscious in less than a minute and dead in five. As deaths go, you could do a lot worse.

REFERENCES:

J. E. Biardi, D. C. Chien, and R. G. Coss, "California ground squirrel (*Spermophilus beecheyi*) defenses against rattlesnake venom digestive and hemostatic toxins." *Journal of Chemical Ecology* 31 (2006), 2501–2518.

H. W. Greene, *Snakes: The Evolution of Mystery in Nature* (Berkeley: University of California Press, 1997).

H. Heatwole and N. S. Poran, "Resistances of sympatric and allopatric eels to sea snake venoms," *Copeia* (1995) 136–147.

M. D. McCue, "Cost of producing venom in three North American pit viper species," *Copeia* (2006), 818–825.

WEIRD SCIENCE: HUMANS DATING CHIMPS

The idea of humans and chimpanzees swapping genes has been around for decades, but a 2006 *Nature* paper* provides hard evidence: "The genome analysis revealed big surprises, with major implications for human evolution," said coauthor and Harvard biologist Eric Lander. The human-chimp speciation occurred slowly, with episodes of hybridization between the emerging species that left a striking impact on the X chromosome. According to Australian anthropologist Colin Groves, species interbred in the wild quite often; even today it could be possible for humans and chimps to have sex and produce offspring, although there would be *ethical problems*.

---

* Patterson, Richter, Gnerre, Lander, and Reich, "Genetic evidence for complex speciation of humans and chimpanzees," *Nature* 441 (2006), 1103–1108.

CHAPTER 10

FATHER KNOWS BEST

Father to son: "Glad I stayed around to father *you*. Doesn't that make you worry?"

Readers share family stories showing that Father Knows Best—except when he doesn't. Darwinian dads play with fire—fireworks, dynamite, gas, and ovens—and with ice, hauling refrigerators and hopping icebergs. These fathers survived, they reproduced, and they can only hope that the offspring did not inherit their questionable judgment!

Father (n.): male who begets children

Papa, pops, daddy, dad, padre, papi, abu, baba, sire, 'rent, progenitor, antecedent, forebearer, paterfamilias, patriarch

Why I'm the Last of Nine Children • My Father, the PhD • Mr. Tinker • Popsicle • Blast from the Past • Volunteer "Fire" Man

Darwin Award Winner:
Why I'm the Last of Nine Children

Unconfirmed Personal Account

Featuring a father, fireworks, vehicles, and a living Darwin!

How my father eliminated himself from the gene pool

My father tried various ways to remove himself from the gene pool. Most methods were mundane: slow suicide by tobacco, alcohol, bad diet. But one incident stands out, caused by Dad's habit of driving down the road while lighting firecrackers off his cigarette. Considering Dad's Darwinian judgment, it was amazing his DNA was so successful.

He enjoyed throwing them out the window as he drove down the street. For convenience he kept the firecrackers in his lap. The fuses were wound together, so he would unwind one, light—throw—*BANG!* Unwind another, light—throw—*BANG!* You get the picture. Uh-huh.

> **Given time, a person such as this can be relied upon to cause himself harm.**

Those who study Darwin know that, given time, a person such as this can be relied upon to cause himself harm. Dear old Dad accidentally added a bounce to his light-throw-*bang* sequence: The firecracker *bounced* off the door and back into his lap! A few firecrackers popped, setting off the remaining firecrackers, and there was some pretty creative driving for a while, amid much smoke and cussing.

I do not know the extent of the damage to Dad's reproductive organs—but I *do* know I was the last of nine children!

Reference: Anonymous daughter

WEIRD SCIENCE: SIX INTRIGUING HUMAN TRAITS

It is not obvious how some aspects of human nature enhance biological success. From the magazine *New Scientist*, some of our quirky foibles that defy explanation:

- Blushing. Charles Darwin himself struggled to explain a response that puts humans at a social disadvantage.
- Laughter.
- Dreams.
- Superstitions.
- Kissing.
- Teenagers. Even the great apes move smoothly from juvenile to adult; why then do humans spend an agonizing decade skulking around in hoodies and ignoring their elders?

At-Risk Survivor: My Father, the PhD

Unconfirmed Personal Account
Featuring a father, fire, a chainsaw, and more

"We have more degrees, but less sense; more knowledge
but less judgment."

—the Dalai Lama

Let an amused daughter tell you about her sire . . .

This weekend was the final straw. Being an extremely cost-conscious person, Dad decided to put half a can of varnish in the toaster oven to liquefy it, as this was the *cheapest* approach. You guessed it—the stuff caught fire! I found him in front of the flaming oven contemplating grabbing the can with his bare hands. Two-foot flames were shooting out of it, causing me to utter a line spoken far too many times in our home:

"What in god's name were you thinking?"

Father's attempts at Darwin fame have included

1. Tipping a small boat while fishing on a lake, nearly drowning my brother and himself. At the time, I thought Mom was being too hard on him when she said it was his own fault that he was in the hospital. I have since revised my judgment.

2. Removing a branch from a locust tree by climbing a ladder with a *running* chainsaw. The branch was not tied off properly, so it fell onto the roof that he was trying to avoid.

3. Rolling a lawn tractor on top of himself by mowing a roadside ditch at a steep angle, resulting in a broken rib—and poison ivy for me, because I spent ten minutes thrashing around in the vegetation while we tried to roll the tractor off Dad. *Again*.

4. Lighting a fire in a basement trash burner *that was not connected to an exhaust pipe*. The fire department loves us.

5. Wandering off to watch the evening news after setting some water to boil in an aluminum Dutch oven. Note that the Merck Index lists the melting point of aluminum as 660°C. When Mom discovered the situation, the sides were glowing bright red, the bottom was melted out, and the kitchen wall was smoking.

A reader who works in the foundry industry warns, "Aluminum does not glow red when it is heated. Molten aluminum does not glow, and that makes it extremely dangerous."

6. Testing the efficacy of old nitroglycerin tablets by swallowing three at once to see if they still worked. I did say he was cheaper, cost conscious. The EMS came to the rescue because his blood pressure had dropped to an undesirable level and he had passed out at the kitchen table. Mere minutes before, he had been planning a drive to the doughnut shop. Thank god he didn't make it to the car before his blood pressure dropped!

He may not yet have used up nine lives, but my father, the PhD, appears to have a running start on Darwin infamy.

Reference: Anonymous daughter

Reader Comments

"Working with PhDs, I'm completely *not* surprised by this . . ."
"I have always said, the more degrees, the dumber."

WENDY'S WORDS OF WISDOM

Most of the chairs in my house are on wheels; I often stood on them to reach high places. One day I read the Darwin Award about a fellow who stood on a rolling chair to fill his bird feeder . . . and rolled right off the twenty-fourth floor balcony. I no longer stand on those chairs in front of windows!

Learn from the mistakes of others.
You won't live long enough to make them all yourself.

At-Risk Survivor: Mr. Tinker

Unconfirmed Personal Account
Featuring a do-it-yourself father

If you ever considered your male parent a doofus, read on.
You might feel better.

My father-in-law tinkers and most often fixes things. I have seen him take apart toasters, motors, electronics, and power washers. He often has several projects on the go. One day he came home with a neighbor's broken microwave and disappeared into his workshop to suss out the problem.

He still tinkers today, but we keep a closer eye on him.

A while later I heard weird noises coming from the workshop, and peeked in. The microwave was now working fine but its front door was missing. The machine was running, and he had his head tucked inside the oven!

I ran in and pulled the plug.

He did not take himself out of the gene pool (not then) but the microwaves may have increased the odds of cancer: A few years later he developed a brain tumor. It was successfully removed and he still tinkers today, but we keep a closer eye on him.

See, there are worse parents . . .

Reference: Anonymous son-in-law

At-Risk Survivor: Popsicle

Unconfirmed Personal Account
Featuring a father, water, alcohol, and a Double Darwin attempt!

In the mid-eighties my father sailed on the research ship *Regina Maris* to study whales in Greenland. One night he noticed there were a lot of icebergs floating by the boat. Icebergs!

After drinking several beers too many with a friend, he and the friend decided to do something stupid. A quick hop onto an iceberg proved that they could stand on it. So my dad decided to hop from iceberg to iceberg with his friend until they reached the nearest village two miles away. Hop after hop, they made their way across the ice floe. As the lights of the village and the shoreline grew nearer, they grew colder and began to pick up the pace.

Alas, in their hurry, they accidentally hopped together onto one small iceberg. It broke under their combined weight, plunging them into the icy salt water where they quickly sobered up.

Dad decided to hop from iceberg to iceberg.

After thrashing about in the ch-ch-chilly water for several interminable minutes, they managed to climb out onto another iceberg, and carefully hopped the rest of the way to shore. The men limped into the village, where they were admitted to the hospital. Treated for hypothermia and a touch of frostbite, and released little worse for the wear, to this day my dad never goes into the ocean.

Reference: Anonymous son

At-Risk Survivor: Blast from the Past

Unconfirmed Personal Account
Featuring a father, an uncle, vehicles, and dynamite!

MID-1950s, USA | My father and my uncle were reminiscing about their youth and shared a rather Darwinian story. In their twenties, they succeeded in assembling one great car out of three junkers. After they accomplished this, they had enough parts left-over to make a second working car—but only barely. This car was missing most of its floorboards, so they could see the ground flash past while driving. They called this a feature rather than a flaw, and decided to have fun with it.

To make the dynamite sticks safer, they shortened the fuses.

In the fifties, high-powered explosives were still easy to acquire. So, with quarter sticks of dynamite at hand, my future father and his brother drove around throwing dynamite through the gaps in the floorboards, and basically scaring the daylights out of people in cars behind them. THIS WAS FUN! They even shortened the fuses to make sure that the sticks would "safely" explode before the car behind them drove over them.

When I heard this story, my first response was, "Weren't you concerned about the gas tank below you?" To my amazement they both looked rather surprised, exchanged glances, and said, "We never thought of that!" My grandfather just laughed and walked out of the room.

Reference: Anonymous son

At-Risk Survivor: Volunteer "Fire" Man

Unconfirmed Personal Account
Featuring fathers, alcohol, explosions, and do-it-yourself!

1978, INDIANA | My friend's father, Mo*, was a volunteer fireman and a home mechanic. He was also a heavy drinker who never seemed to be without booze in his hand. One day I was helping him repair one of their cars. Mo, already well into a six-pack when I arrived, believed that the fuel line was blocked. His solution began with jacking the car up a few feet and draining twelve gallons of gasoline from the tank.

In the process of disconnecting the fuel line from the tank, gasoline spilled all over Mo, soaking his polyester shirt and flooding the floor of the garage. Mo then used several five-gallon buckets to catch the gasoline that was pouring out of the tank. Although the garage door was open to allow ventilation, the fumes were so thick that my friend and I had to step outside to breathe.

Mo continued to lie on the garage floor, in a pool of gasoline under the car.

While we were gulping down fresh air, the water heater, located ten feet from gasoline-soaked Mo, kicked on. Ordinarily this would not be a problem because gasoline fumes are heavy, and the universal building code requires gas-fired tanks to be installed eighteen inches off the floor to prevent accidental combustion. But the circumstances were not ordinary.

---

* Name changed to protect the privacy of the protagonist.

The entire floor went up in flames, and a large fireball came rolling out the garage door toward us. My friend and I dove to the ground to avoid the flames.

After the initial blast, Mo picked himself up and reacted as the trained and experienced firefighter he was—grabbing an extinguisher to put out the flames. Only then did he realize that his polyester shirt had melted to his burned chest. He refused his wife's assistance and, despite his inebriated state, drove himself to the local hospital.

My friend's father lost most of the skin on his chest and most of the hair on his head. He also spent several days in the burn unit and was ultimately tossed out of the volunteer fire department.

Reference: George Leavell

Reader Comment

"This one's for you, Dad. I just hope you're smarter than this when you work on the Studebaker!"

SCIENCE INTERLUDE
DNA FOSSILS: THE EVOLUTION OF HIV

By Kristin Sainani

In 1981, doctors in California and New York reported a baffling new syndrome: Young gay men were dying from a cluster of rare diseases usually seen only in the elderly or those with severe immune deficien-

Phylogenetics: building evolutionary trees based on the genetic similarities between organisms

cies. Doctors were witnessing the first glimpse of a frightening new illness soon to cause worldwide devastation—AIDS.

Amazingly the virus that causes AIDS is not new at all. HIV and its ancestors have plagued mammals for 100 million years. There are no confirmed cases of infection before 1959, and HIV leaves no fossil record, so how do we know so much about the virus's history? Clues to its past lie in its genetic code.

By comparing the genomes of two organisms, scientists can determine when they evolved from a common parent. This detective method, called phylogenetics, tells us, for example, that the DNA sequences of chimpanzees and humans differ by only 2 percent and—

based on the mutation rate—that we shared Thanksgiving dinners with them five to seven million years ago.

But viral evolution takes place on a much faster time scale. Reproducing in days, not decades, with the higher mutation rate of an RNA genome, HIV evolves a million times faster than humans. A fascinating evolutionary history has unfolded in just a single century, and using phylogenetics, scientists have been able to reconstruct this history.

The History of HIV

The AIDS virus (HIV-1 M) first gained a foothold in what is now the city of Kinshasa in the Democratic Republic of the Congo. The city experienced a population explosion in the 1940s that helped the virus build the critical mass it needed to seed a worldwide epidemic. By analyzing samples stored in the early eighties, scientists have shown that the virus traveled from Africa to Haiti around 1966 (likely carried by a single person) and then from Haiti to the U.S. around 1969, twelve years before the first cases were recognized by physicians. Like Haiti, the U.S. happened to be an early stop on the virus's globe trot. HIV spread from the U.S. to Canada and parts of Europe. HIV also spread directly from Africa to Europe and Asia, seeding slightly different strains of the epidemic.

Genetic similarities prove that HIV evolved directly from SIV (simian immunodeficiency virus), which infects African monkeys. SIV was transmitted from monkeys to humans on multiple occasions resulting in several different strains of HIV. One of these strains—HIV-1 M—gave rise to the current global pandemic, while the others remain confined to small groups in Africa. It's clear that

HIV-1 M came from chimpanzees in eastern Cameroon, but it is hotly debated as to when the original transmission occurred. Older studies put the date at about 1930, but a 2008 study shows it was most likely 1908.

In that study, scientists compared the oldest and second-oldest HIV samples: blood (1959) and tissue (1960) from the city of Kinshasa. The HIV gene sequences differed by a whopping 12 percent. Clearly the two strains had diverged from a common ancestor long before 1959. Next, the scientists arranged decades of HIV samples into a genetic tree based on their similarities and converted the genetic distances on the tree into units of time, using the known mutation rate of HIV and some fancy computer modeling. The roots of the tree converged about one hundred years ago.

Between 1884 and 1924, AIDS was born.

> Deadly virulence is the hallmark of a recently evolved disease. Deadly is not a beneficial trait, as killing the host kills the virus. More evolved diseases are less virulent, thus more successful at spreading their genes.

HIV and the Evolutionary Speed Limit

HIV has been evolving for a century, the equivalent of 100 million years of mammalian evolution, so one might expect that HIV would now be an ultra-evolved superbug, even more infectious than the original version. But, surprisingly, most of the genetic changes that have accumulated in the past century are random—driven by genetic drift rather than natural selection.

Genetic drift: genetic changes that accumulate in a species's genome randomly, rather than through natural selection.

HIV is a retrovirus, meaning it stores its genetic information in RNA. Copying RNA back to DNA is a messy, error-prone process. The mutation rate is so high that retroviruses are said to live at the evolutionary speed limit—if they mutated any faster, they would fall apart. So HIV racks up scads of mutations that don't confer an immediate advantage. It's genetic drift is fast enough to be a riptide!

But don't think that HIV doesn't also undergo classic Darwin-style natural selection. HIV is a marvel at escaping the immune system and eluding drugs. There is no better example of natural selection in real time than its evolution within a single host: HIV can change some of its proteins by 25 percent to escape the im-

Protein-coding genes, the part of our DNA that is most obviously useful, makes up less than 2 percent of our genome. There are also RNA coding genes and regulatory DNA. Still, human cells contain a lot of DNA with no known purpose. For instance, the ALU sequence—a 300-nucleotide chunk that repeats ad nauseum—comprises 10 percent of our instruction manual, yet seems to be a useless accident. And a lot of DNA—more than 8 percent—is miscellaneous litter from *alien retroviruses*! By transferring DNA between species, retroviral infections are the Johnny Appleseed of evolution, the Wilt Chamberlain of spreading genes.

mune system and evade drugs—and yet, amazingly, the proteins still function. The virus has made incessant random mutations work in its favor.

HIV tends to revert back to its old form (which is usually more stable) when transmitted to a new host, however, so these mutations aren't preserved at the population level.

Fossils in Our Chromosomes! Prehistoric HIV

There is yet another incredible source of information about HIV evolution: Modern mammals contain clues to its ancient history embedded in their genomes.

You see, when a retrovirus infects a cell, it must insert its genetic material into a chromosome in that cell in order to reproduce. When the virus happens to infect a sex cell, and that sperm or egg becomes a baby, the viral sequence can become a permanent part of the host genome. This DNA "fossil" is called an endogenous (pronounced "en DOJ en iss") retrovirus.

These fossils litter our chromosomes. Scientists estimate that 8.3 percent of the human genome is leftover from retroviral infections—retrovirus DNA trapped in our chromosomes. This is a huge amount of DNA, seven times more than is found in all twenty thousand protein-coding genes in the human genome! (The part of our genome that makes the building blocks of our bodies.)

In 2008, scientists discovered an endogenous lentivirus (the family to which HIV belongs) fossil in the genome of the gray mouse lemur, a small primate found in Madagascar. This discovery shows that HIV's ancestors have been infecting primates for 14 million years. In

2009, scientists discovered a precursor of the lentivirus, an endogenous foamy virus, fossilized in the genome of the sloth. (Think Sid from the movie *Ice Age*.) HIV's ancestors have been infecting mammals for 100 million years—since the age of the dinosaurs!

Startling Conclusion

We now know that our genes are full of alien DNA fossils! We now know the history of the viral scourge known as HIV. Where does it get us? Amazingly a virus that mutates at warp speed hasn't changed much over 100 million years. And those invariant parts that cannot be changed? Good news for vaccine designers, who can exploit these to develop a shot that finally cripples HIV. This is just one of the many practical implications of understanding the evolution of HIV.

REFERENCES:

R. J. Gifford, et al., "A transitional endogenous lentivirus from the genome of a basal primate and implications for lentivirus evolution," *Proceedings of the National Academy of Sciences* 105 (2008), 20362–20367.

M. T. P. Gilbert, et al., "The emergence of HIV/AIDS in the Americas and beyond," *Proceedings of the National Academy of Sciences* 104 (2007), 18566–18570.

A. Katzourakis, "Macroevolution of complex retroviruses," *Science* 325 (2009), 1512.

Paul Sharp and Beatrice H. Hahn, "Prehistory of HIV-1," *Nature* 455 (2008), 605.

M. Worobey, et al., "Direct evidence of extensive diversity of HIV-1 in Kinshasa by 1960," *Nature* 455 (2008), 661–664.

CHAPTER 9

WORKING NINE TO FIVE

If you find yourself thinking, "This tricky shortcut will
save a little time . . ." then you might be headed for a Darwin Award.

Construction, demolition, and all things in between. Whether
you're a professional or a do-it-yourselfer, even a seemingly safe,
sane, straightforward job can turn into a hazard in the hands of
a Darwin Award wannabe. From seasonal ski-lift operator to career safety inspector, *working for a living* takes on a startling new
meaning!

*Wheel of Fortune • Pillar of Strength • A Screw Loose •
Bricks in the Head • Down in the Dumps • Duct Don't*

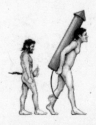

Darwin Award Winner: Wheel of Fortune

Unconfirmed

Featuring work and machismo

WINTER 1995, MICHIGAN | During the ski season at Sugarloaf Resort, a new lift operator assigned to the bottom of Lift 2 was greatly impressed by the bull wheel that turned slowly above his head. The giant spokes on the wheel were impossible to resist. He grabbed a spoke and did a few pull-ups while the wheel turned.

After entertaining himself in this manner for a while, he decided to try this trick on the outer rim of the wheel. His timing was off—he did not drop down in time. Caught between the wheel and the lift cable, he was sliced in twain during his fateful final trip around the bull wheel.

Reference: Anonymous eyewitness

Darwin Award Winner:
Pillar of Strength

Confirmed by Darwin
Featuring work, vehicles, and gravity

9 OCTOBER 2008, SOUTH AFRICA | For days, Johannesburg office workers watched a demolition worker slowly chip away at a pillar supporting the concrete slab above him. One said, "I wondered how they would drop that section." The walls were gone, and only the support pillars remained.

Dozens of observers watched the slow and senseless demolition proceed. Finally the only possible outcome concluded this epic battle. The besieged support collapsed, crushing man and machine beneath a pile of rubble.

The worker, fifty-two, was killed instantly inside the cab of his mini-excavator.

Observers said they had been concerned about the workers' safety for several days. "I cannot believe they did not foresee this," said a shocked witness who did not foresee this. "There was no common sense!"

Reference: thetimes.co.za

Darwin Award Winner:
A Screw Loose

Confirmed by Darwin
Featuring work and falling!

14 APRIL 2008, TEXAS | A contract worker was hired to install reinforcement bars on a communications tower near Camp Bullis. He

"Pride goeth before a fall."
—Proverbs 16:18

was wielding power tools high above the ground, when two other workers saw him lean back and fall 225 feet to his death. Turns out, the man had wrenched loose the bolts on the bar to which he was attached. Police are calling it a tragic accident.

Team Darwin is calling it a "wrenching" accident.

Reference: woai.com

Darwin Award Winner:
Bricks in the Head

Confirmed by Darwin
Featuring work, gravity, and do-it-yourself

30 APRIL 2009, YORK, UNITED KINGDOM | In another do-it-yourself project gone wrong, a forty-one-year-old homeowner attempting to demolish a large brick garden shed succeeded in his primary objective, but suffered collateral damage when the cement-slab roof demolished him.

The unfortunate chap was alone on his property at the time. While one has to question the wisdom of undertaking a demolition project with no one on hand in the event of a mishap, a neighbor happened to witness this "mishap" and immediately summoned help. Hydraulic rams and high-pressure air bags were employed, but it was too late to stop fate. Paramedics pronounced the homeowner dead at the scene.

Speaking to the press, a neighbor described the accident as unspeakable.

In the unequal contest between flesh and stone, the stone always wins.

Reference: York *Evening Press*, thepress.co.uk

Reader Comment

"This could have been on *Renovation Realities Gone Wrong: the Don't DIY* TV show."

At-Risk Survivor: Down in the Dumps

Confirmed by Reliable Eyewitness
Featuring work, insurance, and feces!

2006, UK | During the scrape and resurface of a large residential street in Edinburgh, it was noticed that a large foul sewer ran down the street. As it was believed to be quite shallow, it was necessary to determine its exact route in order to avoid damage by the resurfacing works. Working in a sewer can be dangerous, so three men were sent to an expensive two-week training course, and another six thousand pounds went into the purchase of appropriate equipment: masks, suits, and gas monitors.

Once the project was under way, the supervising engineer decided to pop along one afternoon and see how work was commencing. The tent covering the sewer was shaking and bulging oddly. He threw open the flaps and was presented with the unsavory sight of three men wrestling over the open manhole, covered in waste matter! Two were shouting at a third, who was unconscious, drenched in waste, and not breathing.

What was going on?

The civil engineer, trained in resuscitation techniques, began the unappealing process of clearing the unconscious man's airway. Fortunately at that point the man started breathing again and immediately vomited a stream of waste. The ambulance was summoned—and then it was time for 'splaining.

Remember the training course? Remember the

expensive new gear? Dumb, Dumber, and Dumbest decided that that was all too much effort. The sewer was so close to the surface, they figured that it would be easier to simply hang one of them head first with a torch to see the lay of the line. They held an arm-wrestling contest, and the loser was flipped upside down and lowered into the narrow manhole.

Immediately he was overcome by the fumes and passed out. With no shout to stop, Dumb and Dumber continued to lower Dumbest until he was immersed up to his shoulders in the pooling waste. After a minute or so with no response, they pulled him up and realized what had happened. They were both fighting to administer CPR when their supervisor arrived.

All four men received injections to ward off infection. Dumbest was kept in the hospital for further treatment. He developed a nasty mouth infection that caused him to lose teeth, but he survived. Denied Darwin Awards, the three men subsequently decided to try for a Stella Award*: Dumb, Dumber, and Dumbest filed an insurance claim against their company for injury and trauma, as their shortcut was not specifically forbidden in the method statement! The company settled out of court.

Reference: Disillusioned engineer

---

* The Stella Awards recognize the most frivolous civil lawsuits, such as the diabetic obese man who sued McDonald's. www.StellaAwards.com

Reader Comments

"Shitty job."

"Even the best-trained people do stupid things."

"Pass this along to your crews, this is *not* the correct way
to inspect a sewage leakage!"

"See what happens when you have an employee manual?"

"An unsavory example of sue-age."

DARWIN AWARD WINNER: MAN MEETS MANURE

At least the Dunkin' Donut man survived his disgusting dip. In a
case of man-meets-manure, twenty-three-year-old Benjamin
lost his life in 1999 in one of the most unappetizing manners
possible when he careened into a 400,000-gallon tank of raw
sewage. He was apparently driving too fast to make the sharp
turn in front of the wastewater treatment plant, as his
momentum carried him through a chain link fence, across an
easement, and past a low post-and-rail fence surrounding the
tank of decomposing sewage. Divers located his body beside
his Mazda pickup, at the bottom of the sixteen-foot-deep tank.

Reference: *Darwin Awards: Evolution in Action* (Plume, 2001)

At-Risk Survivor: Duct Don't

Confirmed by Reliable Eyewitness
Featuring work and gravity!

DECEMBER 2009, CANADA | Lester*, a career fire-safety in-
spector, entered a building in downtown Alberta for its annual fire
inspection. Although new to the building, Lester is not new to his
job. With several degrees in Fire and Health Safety, and fluent in
three languages, this all-around nice guy has expertly inspected
buildings around the world for many years.

The structure he entered has a mechanical room in the bowels
of the building, a "boiler room" with a vast air duct that feeds into
the air filters. The duct itself is more than strong enough to support
the weight of a man. Indeed, inspectors are
required to climb onto the duct from a cat-
walk on the floor above, in order to inspect
one of the fire extinguishers.

**Oh, the Darwin
Awards that have
resulted from time-
saving shortcuts.**

Lester had just inspected that very safety
device and was standing on top of the air
duct when he decided to save himself a few minutes of time. Oh, the
Darwin Awards that have resulted from time-saving shortcuts. The
nearby fire device was almost in range if he stretched!

A highly trained Fire and Safety Inspector—well, it's his or her
job to know how to inspect a building safely. But sometimes the

---

* Name changed to protect the privacy of the protagonist.

safe route is *inconvenient*. Instead of traveling all the way back down to the basement and climbing a ladder, Lester decided to

A. climb down the side of the air duct,

B. in nearly complete darkness,

C. despite being warned by his senior partner an hour earlier that he definitely should not climb on the ductwork.

Halfway down, he misjudged his footing . . . and gravity performed its civic duty. Lester plummeted ten feet to the cement ground, landing in the carpentry shop adjacent to the boiler room and punching a hole through a tile ceiling in the process.

Sometimes the safe route is inconvenient.

Lester survived with two broken ankles, but easily could have impaled himself had he landed to either side—on the table saw or the tool bench.

Reference: D. Gustafson, First Aid Responder

Reader Comment

"An Inconvenient ~~Truth~~ Route."

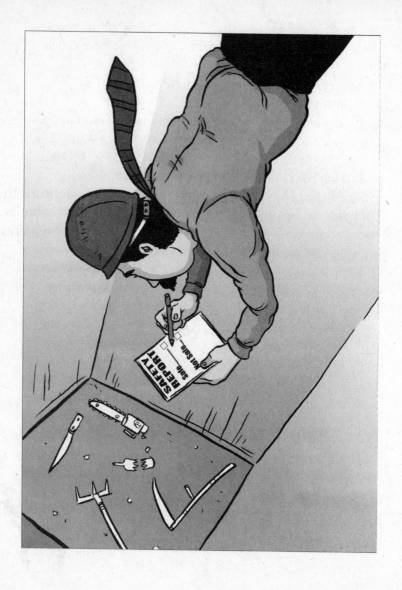

SCIENCE INTERLUDE
RNAI: INTERFERENCE
BY MOTHER NATURE

By Alison Davis

When was the last time you were happy about a flub-up?

In the unvarnished world of science, a wrong result can be the best thing that ever happened, but that success isn't always immediately obvious. Thus is the case for the discovery of the game-changing, paradigm-busting, gene-silencing process called RNA interference, or RNAi.

To be fair, RNAi isn't exactly new, and it wasn't just discovered. Like so many stories in science, the epic tale of RNAi is one of hard work, some blind luck, and a careful eye for the unexpected.

RNA Rules

Thanks to the Human Genome Project and subsequent discoveries, DNA is a household name. Less famous, but also part of our genetic material, is RNA. You can't see either of these stringy molecules, even with a very powerful scope, but both consist of long chains of four molecular "letters" (GATC or GAUC) hooked together by sugar molecules.

Yet despite being made of similar ingredients, DNA and RNA are quite different. This is because DNA uses a different sugar than RNA (deoxyribose versus ribose) to join its alphabet. DNA is rigid and stable, double-stranded, and assumes a beautiful staircaselike structure. RNA is floppy and unstable, usually single-stranded, and sometimes tangles up into knots. These sister molecules have completely different personalities.

Researchers have known for decades that DNA stores our body plans—genetic information that is passed on through generations. They thought that RNA was merely a middleman, helping translate the DNA into proteins that do most of the work in the body. (If DNA is the blueprint, proteins are both contractors and building materials.) But it is time for mighty DNA to move aside. Beginning with the discovery of RNAi, researchers now realize that RNA is at least as important as DNA, if not more so.

The notion that RNA is as important as DNA contradicts the traditional paradigm we are taught in school. *But it's true!* RNA is headed for Warhol's fifteen minutes of fame.

New types of RNA seem to appear monthly: snRNA, piRNA, and many more; microRNAs are the powerful "transcription factors" of eighties' fame. Noncoding RNAs are about to turn the definition of a *gene* on its head!

Running Interference

RNAi is a natural gene-silencing process that has been preserved as a survival tool throughout billions of years of evolution. This gene-silencing effect was described decades ago—after a series of frustrating failed experiments—and today, at long last, its mechanism is known. **RNAi brutally hijacks a special form of RNA** that is doubled up, cleverly termed double-stranded RNA, and chops it into bits like a serial killer getting rid of a body!

This is useful to the cell in many ways. For example, double-stranded RNA, otherwise rare, is a common component of many viruses. Virus-infected plants sense the wrongful presence of double-stranded RNA, and set RNAi in motion—recruiting a series of protein machines to interfere with the rogue invader's dastardly plans by slicing up its genes.

Interfere is too gentle a term since RNAi works through a molecular machine, descriptively named *dicer,* that cleaves double-stranded RNA into much smaller pieces. Those broken fragments are worse than useless to the virus, because they stick to other viral RNAs, gumming up their ability to schedule production time on protein-making ribosome factories.

RNAi *dicer* destroys viral RNA; no RNA means no new viruses and a healthy plant.

Today, researchers have unearthed RNAi in virtually every organism, from plants to pandas to people. The payoff is a revolution in medical research, leading the way to cures and treatments for a wide range of troublesome diseases.

Tough Tobacco and the Petunia Boondoggle

The RNAi epic begins in 1928 with, of all things, tobacco.

As published in the wildly popular *Journal of Agricultural Research*, a scientist who infected a tobacco seedling with the deadly tobacco ring-spot virus didn't succeed in knocking it off (and this was years before we knew the evils of smoking). Try as he might, this researcher could not kill the plant with a supposedly deadly virus. Repeated infections had only a minuscule effect, shriveling the plant's bottom leaves. Wha . . . ? Why was it stubbornly thriving? What was protecting this tough tobacco?

Fast-forward more than a half century and now the patient is a petunia. The protagonists are two plant researchers aiming to beef up the petunia's drab purpleness by giving it a scientific booster shot of color. In molecular-speak, they were supplementing the purple petunia with an additional pigmentation gene.

Well, it didn't work out. Adding this "purpling gene" did not beef up the petunia's purpleness. Instead the puzzled plant scientists discovered that more is *less*, and their gene-gineered petunia flowers were plain-Jane white, or at best, splotchy. The hell . . . ? Why are the petunias white? What a boondoggle!*

------

* Researchers were trying to determine whether chalcone synthase (CHS) was the rate-limiting enzymatic step in anthocyanin biosynthesis, the pathway that makes petunias purple. They *overexpressed* CHS DNA in petunias, expecting more purple, or no change—but instead got white or splotchy flowers. They measured CHS protein levels; the levels were far *lower* than normal, confounding common sense! Thus, from a failed experiment, the hypothesis of gene silencing was born.

Oblivious to the commercial windfall of dye-ready petunias, the curious researchers plodded on, searching fruitlessly for a reason behind this perplexing failure.

Smashed Dogma?

The frustrating dilemma in both instances was that the results seemingly violated scientific dogma, firmly established before we were born!

Math–religion guru Gregor Mendel worked alone in his bucolic monastery, making history with simple equipment available to any 1800s gardener. Mendel deciphered the rules for how genes from two pea parents combine, then transmit traits to their offspring. Today, Mendelian genetics explain why your hair is as frizzy and unruly as your mother's and her father's.

Mendel's laws form the basis of modern genetics and are the motive behind today's $40 billion biotech industry. But the petunia just didn't fit. The experimental results did not follow Mendel's laws. Oh no-sies! Talk about a fast track to career failure.

But it was not quite as intractable as an NP-Complete problem.*

---

* NP-Complete describes a large class of problems in computer science. The good news is that a solution to any one of them would provide a solution to all; the bad news is that in forty years, no one has found a solution to even one. NP-Complete problems are often easy to identify, and once a problem is shown to fall in this possibly impossible category, the researcher is spared a frustrating wild goose chase. UC–Santa Cruz professor Scott Brandt often tells his students of his last days in industry, when his boss asked him to solve a

The answer arrived, although it took its own sweet time. This time, it is the 1990s and a new set of researchers are focused on the age-old mystery, "How do genes drive muscle development in roundworms as they grow in a petri dish?"

The worm scientists' plan was to use a biotech trick to wipe out a particular worm muscle gene and witness what happens to the worms without that gene. But the scientists ran into a snag. Results were the opposite of expected! Adding a "control blank" (RNA that was *supposed* to do nothing) also wiped out the gene. Arghhh. What in tarnation was going on?

This time, perseverance paid off. A series of carefully planned tests explained the impossible result and finally unveiled the workings—mechanism, gears, and cogs—of gene silencing. *It was RNAi.* Earning the 2006 Nobel Prize for their work, Dr. Andrew Z. Fire and Dr. Craig C. Mello revealed that RNA itself, folded into a double-stranded knot, was the trigger for RNAi to shut down specific genes.

Now it all made sense.

RNAi to the Rescue: Making Sense of Petunias

In the Case of The Purple Petunia, the purple pigment gene *would* have obeyed Mendel's rules, but that gene was being ignored: Its

---

difficult problem. He quickly determined that the problem was NP-Complete, and that no solution would be forthcoming. His boss said, "That's not good enough. Work on it some more!" Shortly thereafter, the frustrated professor returned to the academic life.

RNA messenger had been *chopped into bits* by RNAi. In the Case of The Virus-Resistant Tobacco, RNAi *diced up* the menacing ring-spot virus, a virus that otherwise would have stunted and killed the plant.

Molecular biologists are now convinced that RNAi protects things that can't run away, like a tobacco plant. But they are less clear on the biological reasons for RNAi to exist in mammals, including us. One theory—backed by a mounting arsenal of evidence—is that RNAi serves as guardian of our genome by restricting the philandering of traveling viruses and other mobile segments of DNA that might go cavorting from one place to another. **RNAi: Guardian of Our Genome** Genes in the wrong place create big messes—including many diseases—and RNAi may be our body's way of keeping things tidy.

RNAi: The gene broom, sweeping away suspicious fragments of RNA.

Imagine! What might RNAi be enlisted to do?

Imagine how many wonderful things we can do with a tool that destroys target genes!

Scientists are learning to use RNAi as a tool to eliminate the genes we dread, in tumors, diseased cells, HIV infections, and so forth. Imagine RNAi used as a specific and safe natural pesticide! Imagine custom RNAi sprays that eradicate crop infections, slaughter mosquitoes, or make tastier lettuce! And admit it, couldn't lettuce use a tasty-spray?

Maybe it's time to revisit the purple petunia.

REFERENCES:

D. Baulcombe, "RNA silencing in plants (Review)," *Nature* 431 (2004), 356–363.

National Institute of General Medical Science, "RNA interference fact sheet," http://www.nigms.nih.gov/News/Extras/RNAi/factsheet.htm.

G. L. Sen and H. M. Blau, "A brief history of RNAi: The silence of the genes (Review)," *FASEB* 9 (2006), 1293–1299.

The 2006 Nobel Prize in Physiology or Medicine, "Advanced information, RNA Interference," http://nobelprize.org/nobel_prizes/medicine/laureates/2006/adv .html.

CHAPTER 8

PRIVATE PARTS: CAUGHT WITH THEIR PANTS DOWN

"A friend told me, when I get depressed, just look up the Darwin Awards and I will feel better. Boy was he right!"

Placing one's privates in predicaments is a common fast track to a Darwin Award. We lead off with two stories regarding scatology, follow up with two rare "living winners," and end with four suspicious sex acts. Darwin delivers well-deserved kudos to the creatively kinky!

Dying to Go • Short Circuit • Muffled Explosion •
Bitter Biter Bit a Nitwit • Bench Press • Pipe Cleaner •
Single Bud Vase • Battered Sausages

Also see Tennessee Pee, p. 184,
and Rub the Mint, p. 199.

Darwin Award Winner: Dying to Go

Confirmed by Darwin
Featuring urine, alcohol, and falling!

12 APRIL 2008, FLORIDA | Traffic was moving slowly on south-bound I-95. Shawn M. had recently left a Pompano Beach bar, and now he was stuck in traffic. As the saying goes, you don't buy beer—you just rent it, and Shawn couldn't wait another moment to relieve himself. "I need to take a leak," he told his friends.

Traffic was deadlocked, so the waterlogged man climbed out, put his hand on the divider, and jumped over the low concrete wall for a little privacy . . . only to fall sixty-five feet to his death. "He probably thought there was a road, but there wasn't," said a Fort Lauderdale police spokesman. The car was idling on an overpass above the railroad lines.

His mother shared her thoughts. "Shawn didn't do a whole lot for a living. He got along on his charm, just like his father." Though his death was tragic, Shawn's downfall proves the old adage: *Look before you leak!*

Reference: *South Florida Sun Sentinel; The Miami Herald*

Reader Comments

"Guess he was dying to go."
"He shoulda peed in a bottle."

"That's why they call it Flori-duh."

"Apparently it was just his time to go."

"Now here's a wee joke."

"I wonder if he wet his pants from fright!"

At-Risk Survivor:
Look Before You Leak

In a related story, a personal account, this time not fatal . . .

SUMMER 2003, USA | "I hired several laborers to prepare a garden area for me. They needed some supplies, so I showed them the location of ice water and the bathroom, and left to obtain the supplies. Upon my return, I found an ambulance in front of my home, along with two police cars. The police informed me that the neighbor had dialed 911 to report a naked man screaming and running around the yard.

My yard!

As it turned out, one of the laborers had needed to answer the call of nature. Rather than use the indoor bathroom, he went into the woods behind the house, dropped his trousers, and squatted down—right on top of a nest of hornets! He was released from the hospital about a week later, having learned a very painful and nearly fatal lesson: *Always watch* where you go!

"Watch where you are going— and look before you leak!"

Reference: Cy Stapleton

Darwin Award Winner:
Short Circuit

Confirmed by Darwin

Featuring feces, a criminal, and electricity

MARCH 1989, SOUTH CAROLINA | Michael Anderson Godwin was a lucky murderer whose death sentence had been commuted to life in prison. Ironically he was sitting on the metal toilet in his cell and attempting to fix the TV set when he bit down on a live wire—and electrocuted himself!

Ironie des Schicksals (Irony of Fate)

Reference: News of the Weird, Gizmodo.com

Reader Comments

"I suppose he ended up in the netherworld."

"His last name predicted his fate: God wins."

Darwin Award Winner: Muffled Explosion

Confirmed by Darwin

Featuring gonads, explosions, machismo, and a living Darwin!

10 JANUARY 2009, PENNSYLVANIA | An embarrassed and seriously injured seventeen-year-old initially claimed that an explosive had been planted in his backpack by persons unknown. However, police investigators soon extracted the truth. He had found an M-80 explosive at his grandmother's house, taken it to his room to "examine" it, and began to repeatedly light and extinguish the fuse.

During one of these cycles the fuse would not go out, so he jammed the red cardboard tube between his thighs and covered it with his hand to muffle the explosion. This plan was less successful than he had hoped.

One loud *KABOOM!* later, our junior pyrotechnics specialist had lost his right hand and right leg. It is not known whether the injury also affected his ability to repro-

Commonly thought to be a quarter stick of dynamite, M-80s (according to pyrouniverse.com) actually contain 1/50 the amount of explosive (3 grams) and use flash powder rather than TNT. Used by the U.S. military to simulate grenade explosions, M-80s were outlawed in 1966 under the Child Protection Act. They are not safe enough to be detonated by the average man on the average street, let alone by an average seventeen-year-old in an average bedroom.

duce, but if it had, the fellow would be eligible to compete for the honor of a living Darwin Award.

Reference: WPXI News; *Pittsburgh Tribune-Review*; pittsburghlive.com; *Pittsburgh Post-Gazette*

Reader Comments

"A new way to lose weight."

"Stupidity, thy name is teenager!"

"A glimpse of America's youth at its finest."

WEIRD SCIENCE: BAND-AIDS!

Good news for competitors during their Darwin Awards tryouts!

Those competing for a Darwin Award often suffer a few nicks and dings along the way. Recently scientists designed medical sutures made from natural polymer excreted by helpful bacteria. Sutures made from these fibers are naturally absorbed by our bodies, so no more pulling stitches! Doctors report favorably on the flexible and easy-to-work-with sutures.

Bacterial polymers: a perfect human repair material.

"Those whom life does not cure, death will."

—Cormac McCarthy

Urban Legend: Bitter Biter Bit a Nitwit

Unconfirmed—Suspected Urban Legend
Featuring gonads and a raccoon!

Although this story was submitted dozens of times—citing news articles from Belgium, Denmark, Norway, Italy, Japan, and Australia—we classify this story as an urban legend, because the sole source of all these news reports is *The Sun* tabloid. If you have a reliable source confirming the story, please contact Darwin. www.DarwinAwards.com/contact

JANUARY 2009, RUSSIA | A RAGING RACCOON HAS BITTEN OFF A PERVERT'S PRIVATES AS HE WAS TRYING TO RAPE THE ANIMAL, screams the headline. When most of us see a wild animal, raping it never enters our minds. Why would it?

Alexander, forty-four, was on a drunken weekend with friends in Moscow when he leapt on the terrified animal. "When I saw the raccoon I thought I'd have some fun," he told stunned casualty surgeons.

Although there was not much left to work with, plastic surgeons were trying to reconstruct his mangled manhood. If he is unable to procreate—he is eligible for a Darwin Award. But thus far no reports have "leaked" on the success of the shaft graft.

Reference: thesun.co.uk; FailBlog.org photo of a newspaper clipping

<u>**Reader Comments**</u>

"I hope it doesn't work—I'm an animal lover."

"Next time try a beaver."

<u>URBAN LEGEND: RACCOON ROCKET</u>

Raccoons seem to be nuclei around which Urban Legends condense. For example, in rural Pennsylvania a group of men were drinking beer and discharging firearms at a raccoon that was wandering by. The animal escaped into a three-foot-diameter drainage pipe. Determined to smoke the animal out, one man retrieved a can of gasoline and poured some down the pipe. After several unsuccessful attempts to ignite the fuel, the determined dude proceeded to slide feet first, fifteen feet down the sloping pipe to toss the match. The subsequent rapidly expanding fireball propelled him back the way he had come, though at a much higher rate of speed. He exited the angled pipe "like a Polaris missile," according to a witness, with "a Doppler effect to his scream as he flew over his house, followed by a loud thud" as he landed on his own front lawn.

Reference: *Darwin Awards:*
Evolution in Action (Plume, 2001)

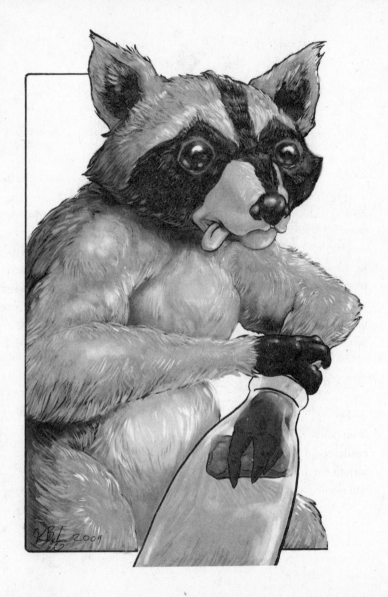

At-Risk Survivor: Bench Press

Confirmed by Darwin

Featuring gonads!

6 AUGUST 2008, HONG KONG | It's raining. You're lonely. Why not? That was how forty-one-year-old Le Xing found himself facedown on a bench and calling for help in the middle of the night.

The lonely man had noticed that the steel sit-up benches in a local park had numerous ventilation holes and thought it might be possible to use them for sexual gratification.

Once Le Xing became aroused, he found he was stuck and could not remove himself from the hole in the bench. Quite understandably, he panicked. Police received a call from a disturbed man and arrived to find him trapped facedown on the bench.

Facedown on a bench and calling for help in the middle of the night . . .

Doctors were summoned to the scene. They tried everything, but eventually, emergency workers had to cut the entire bench free and take both it and him to the hospital.

Four painful hours later, doctors finally separated man from bench. It is certainly possible that the lack of blood flow easily could have caused sufficient damage to require doctors to remove his penis. This is one bad date that Le Xing will never forget.

Reference: telegraph.co.uk, weirdasiannews.com, asylum.com, news.ninemsn.com.au

Reader Comments

"What a pre'dic'ament!"

"Wholly embarrassing."

"A man from the country that invented the Chinese Finger Trap should have been able to figure out how to release his piece, ya think?"

"Apparently this man has never heard of Vaseline."

"Talk about a 'Man of Steel'!"

"Polishing the bench."

"That's what happens when you the use services of a 'cheap ho.'"

A photograph of the man and his metal mistress:
www.DarwinAwards.com/book/benchpress

At-Risk Survivor:
Pipe Cleaner

Confirmed by Darwin
Featuring gonads!

5 JANUARY 2010, SOUTHAMPTON, UK | Oh dear. Yet another man has got his hoohaw stuck in a pipe, taking many precise maneuvers with a blowtorch and metal grinder to cut him loose from the steel—might as well say it—Iron Maiden. All told, seven fire-fighters and medics were involved in the delicate operation. "The crew was worried about things getting too hot during the cutting," said a tongue-in-cheek spokesman for Hampshire Fire and Rescue.

Reference: *The Sun, Daily Telegraph*

As long-time readers know, this isn't the first man caught laying pipe . . . but not all pipe incidents are lascivious. For instance, check out Mortar Fire, page 155.

At-Risk Survivor: Single Bud Vase

Confirmed by Reliable Eyewitness
Featuring gonads!

2009 | I am a nurse on a busy surgical unit. I received a report that a young patient was arriving with severe lacerations to his unmentionables. Try as I might, I could not imagine what this poor lad had done to injure himself.

"You stuck *what where?*"

The twenty-one-year-old patient confided to me that, upset by his girlfriend's unwillingness to have intimate relations, he had romanced a flower vase! Alas, in the heat of the moment, the bud vase shattered, lacerating his penis. He required emergency surgery.

Afterward, the urologist told us that the boy would require a catheter for weeks, and he was unsure if his mojo would be functional. I felt sorry for the kid . . . but did laugh when I saw his girlfriend walking down the hall, bringing flowers!

Reference: A Nurse who wishes to remain anonymous

Reader Comments

"A new technique for Kenny . . . !"
(This *Southpark* cartoon character frequently
dies in freak masturbation accidents.)

At-Risk Survivor: Battered Sausages

Confirmed by Reliable Eyewitness
Featuring gonads, mostly!

Dr. Kiernan has been a prolific contributor to the Darwin Awards, particularly with urological reports. Four stories from the files of the good doctor . . .

MARCH 2007 | The most grateful patient I ever treated had found true love with a household vacuum. He presented to me with a very swollen and sorry-for-itself penis, and it was obvious that the member had been somewhere it shouldn't be. I confronted him, and he denied the truth (wouldn't you?) until I told him I had a foolproof cure to prevent recurrent damage. He brightened up.

"Make sure to attach a cardboard toilet-paper roll to the end of the suction first, so you can soak the roll off your happy peewee if it becomes necessary." He was most grateful for the advice.

At-Risk Survivor: What a Pickle!

APRIL 2008 | Our hero sought my urgent professional attention after an accident involving a car and his motorbike, on his way to a Saturday night party. He had sustained a compound broken femur. The management of this life-threatening condition was hampered by his refusal to have his black leather trousers cut off. In fact, we argued with him for ten minutes trying to access his common sense and get his consent, while doing other necessary things to help him medically, of course. As it turned out, it wasn't the expense of the leather trousers with which he was so preoccupied . . . It was our imminent discovery of the large cucumber in his underwear! Mom always warned us, "Wear clean underwear in case you get hit by a car." Here's a new one for Mom to worry about. This gambit is far from unusual. In the rougher parts of outer Sydney no one would want to be reincarnated as a cucumber because . . . well . . . !

At-Risk Survivor: Fishing Tackle

SEPTEMBER 2008 | *Daily Telegraph* reported that a small fish had found its way into the urethra of a fourteen-year-old boy. The patient was admitted to the hospital with complaints of pain, dribbling, and urinary retention. Floundering for a rationale for his predicament, the boy's dubious account was that he was cleaning the fish tank in his house and was holding a fish in his hand when he needed to use the toilet. While he was passing urine, the two-cm fish supposedly slipped from his hand and entered his urethra, say Drs. Vezhaventhan and Jeyaraman, who wrote a paper on the unfortunate fish and boy.

At-Risk Survivor: A Bit Potty

1960S | My father, also a doctor, treated a man who rode his bicycle six miles one rainy evening to seek advice at the local English hospital. He wore a large, dark raincoat which he refused to remove for the nursing staff. In privacy, he did so for my father, who was most surprised. This surprise did not emanate from the fact that the man had got himself stuck in an old-fashioned clay urinal, but that he had cycled six miles with it hanging from the end of his penis! Needless to say Dad didn't buy the story of being caught while having a wee. This ended rather badly, I am afraid. Dad claims there was no other way but to break it out with a hammer.

Could this man thus be a historic Darwin Awardee?

Reference: Dr. Davida Kiernan

SCIENCE INTERLUDE
WHY BOTHER WITH SEX?

By Alice Cascorbi

Not the complaint of a tired housewife or the sour grapes of a frustrated "playah," but rather a real dilemma for evolutionary biologists. If an organism's purpose is to propagate its own DNA, why waste time and energy searching for a mate? If its unique genetic code lets it survive and flourish, why dilute that code with another creature's genes?

"But don't we need sex to make babies?"

Sure, *we* do. But step outside our species to recognize the big difference between sex (exchanging genes) and reproduction (making offspring). The entire kingdom Prokaryota would consider us perverts if we could explain to them how sex and reproduction coincide within our multicellular selves. Any proper prokaryote would tell you that sex—sharing genes—is something one does with multiple partners, trading bits of DNA via cell-connecting tubes or viral vectors. Reproduction, OTOH, means privately splitting your single-celled self into two identical organisms.

Strawberries, Sharks, and Komodo Dragons

Asexual reproduction is actually so common that we barely think about it. Every time you pull a strawberry sucker from your garden or trim a spider plant's spiders, you're dealing with asexual reproduction. Bananas, the notoriously phallic fruit, are seedless and propagate by rooting cuttings. And even garlic, that spicy aphrodisiac, reproduces without sex via bulbs.

> All-female clones can continue to reproduce indefinitely, but all-male clones are extinct after one generation. Asexuality can be a dead end!

And it's not just plants. Many worms and insects, a boatload of coelenterates (pronounced *see LEN' ter ates'*—sea anemones and jellyfish), and even some fish and lizards reproduce asexually. Female sharks raised in captivity have given birth to all-female young whose DNA comes only from their virgin mothers. Ditto for Komodo dragons, except that through a genetic twist, their offspring are all male. Parthenogenesis has been reported as far up the evolutionary ladder as the domestic turkey.

Why Do Without? The Cost of Sex

Sex always costs—not necessarily in money, but in the more primal currencies of energy, time, and exposure to danger. Exhausting fights over mates raise the cost of business in the sexual world—ask any stag during rutting season. And consider over-the-top mating displays like the nine-foot blossom of the carrion flower, the peacock's tail feathers, or the human's silly, showy "peacock" brain. (See "Sex on the Brain," p. 109 for a treatise on human brains and runaway sexual selection.)

Elaborate mating structures take time and energy to make and increase exposure to predators ♠ as well as potential mates. ♀ A peacock's huge tail feathers slow him down; the leopard who pounces on a poky peacock is reaping a cheap lunch subsidized by the cost of sex—fancy plumage—to her prey. Time spent attracting a mate could be spent feeding, gathering energy, and growing clones. Nonsexual creatures avoid all that mating hassle by just doing it solo.

Lesbian Lizards

The most fascinating sex-free creatures are the ones who have given up sex after enjoying it for millions of years. There are all-female species of whiptail lizard, blue-spotted salamander, and topminnow. Tellingly, all of these species have mating behaviors that show their recent evolution from sexual ancestors. All-female blue-spotted salamanders mate with males of related species; the sperm triggers development of their eggs, but contributes no genes. The live-bearing desert topminnow, *Poeciliopsis lucidus,* does the same.

Whiptail lizards of the desert Southwest go one step further: Members of the all-female species *Cnemidophorus uniparens* take on male-like behavior and mate with other females in a process called pseudocopulation. Their female-on-female behavior stimulates egg production and the birth of clones.

If so many organisms get along fine without sex, why are the rest of us still doing it? Especially, note evolutionists dryly, when mathematical models show that asexual females should take over any population within fifty generations, due to the time and energy they save.

But—that's fifty generations without *natural selection*—with no new trends in weather, no new diseases, no new tricks by your predators. Do you see the problem?

Nature is *never* free of natural selection. Even when the physical environment is stable, the ecosystem of predators and pathogens is not. You are food for them, and if there is one thing stronger than the sex drive, it is the need to feed. Even Darwin would agree: *You must survive until you can pass on your genes.* Food comes before sex, and organisms will do anything to get it—or avoid becoming it—even swap genes. If everyone else is swapping genes in an arms race to eat you, and you're standing there having sex with yourself, you're falling behind.

In a nutshell, sex is an engine of diversity: More varieties of organisms are birthed when they are conceived with a partner. A family of clones is obviously less diverse than a family with mixed genes. And when your genotype is the delicious flavor of the day, you'll want to make sure your offspring are something your predators have never tasted before. Whether you need faster legs, a longer tongue, or slimier skin—sex is the way to go.

Now that the case has been made in favor of sex, how do creatures get by without it? If a hungry world is chasing them, why do lesbian lizards have any place in nature?

Studies show that asexual plants and animals thrive in marginal environments with little competition, but cannot compete with sexual relatives in mainstream habitats. Asexual butterflies flutter on alpine mountaintops, asexual plants pop up in plowed fields and after volcanic eruptions, and asexual vertebrates make their homes where it's hot, icy, or dry. Note that the all-female species mentioned above are the *desert* topminnow and lizards of the *desert* Southwest. These asexual desert creatures have close relatives living in more appealing climates—lounging on beaches, soaking in tropical pools—who reproduce using sex.

In a marginal habitat, it pays to pass on to your children your proven genotype, unchanged. Only a few things can live where you live, and on balance, it's best to stick with the tried and true. And saving energy with low-cost solo reproduction is a big help too.

Asexuals live where the environment allows natural selection to slow down.

#1 Reason for Sex: Aliens!

OK, then—since sex is a choice, why choose sex?*

Field studies indicate that the number one reason for sex is biological interactions between species. Mainstream habitats are rich in predators, pathogens, and parasites. Sex, by shuffling genes, is especially good at protecting against parasites and dis-

---

* Sex is a choice a species can make, an evolutionary path a species can take. We do not intend to imply that *any* creature can choose between sexual or asexual reproduction modes. Having learned to clone mammals, humans have become the first creature that is able to make this choice on an individual, conscious basis.

Japanese knotweed, *Polygonum cuspidatum*, a handsome but rather unwelcome invasive weed, is one of the first to colonize fresh lava fields in its native Japan. Its ability to flex sexual and non-sexual generations is its strength as a hardy colonizer. A single asexual clone of Japanese knotweed is now invading northern Europe. Although this clone would not stand a chance back home, far from its native pests and predators—the weed is nearly invincible—See Bailey, Bímová, and Mandák, "Asexual spread versus sexual reproduction and evolution in Japanese Knotweed," *Biological Invasions* 11, no. 5 (2009).

ease. Studies in the lab—evolution in a bottle—show that those odd creatures that switch between sexual and asexual reproduction, like the water snail, *Potomopyrgus antipodarum*, get sexy when their parasites start hopping.

You see, it's the tiniest "predators" that evolve the fastest. Compare the life cycle of a flea (four weeks) to its prey, your cat, or compare a human life span to the two-week flu virus life cycle. Pathogens have many extra generations for natural selection to work, so they quickly hone in on the genetic weaknesses of, well, *you*. Prey must evolve, shift genetic profiles, to combat these enemies. Evolutionary biologists call this the "Red Queen Hypothesis" and liken the costly persistence of sexual reproduction to the Lewis Carroll character who had to keep running to stay in place.

Dandelions

Both sexual and asexual lifestyles have their niches, and a great example lives as close as your backyard.

In their native Eurasia dandelions grow as normal flowers, producing male pollen carried by bees to fertilize female ovules. But dandelions have also evolved asexual lines that clone themselves and send out seeds containing identical DNA. The "old sod" in Europe is golden with sexual dandelions, but it is the asexual ones that have blanketed the virgin continent of North America. They are a beautiful example of just when asexual reproduction is best. Far from their native pests and pathogens, sex-free dandelions have colonized every lawn in the USA because they are able to spread faster than their sexual relatives—even while wasting energy producing cheery yellow flowers that no bee will ever fertilize.

So the next time you're in the mood to mate, stop and consider an alternative used by bananas, bacteria, lizards, and sharks. Maybe it is better to close the curtains and just do it yourself.

REFERENCES:

Crews, Grassman, and Lindzey, "Behavioral facilitation of reproduction in sexual and unisexual whiptail lizards," *Proc Nat Acad Sci USA* 83 (1986), 9547–9550.

Juliet Eilperin, "Female Sharks Can Reproduce Alone, Researchers Find." *The Washington Post,* http://tinyurl.com/2aaau4

Lively, Craddock, and Vrijenhoek, "Red Queen hypothesis supported by parasitism in sexual and clonal fish," *Nature* 344 (1990), 864–866.

Lively and Joleka, "Temporal and spatial distributions of parasites and sex in a freshwater snail," *Evolutionary Ecology Research* 4 (2002), 219–226.

Thomas F. Savage, "A Guide to Recognition of Parthenogenesis in Incubated Turkey Eggs," Oregon State University (2008), http://tinyurl.com/y56s4xj

CHAPTER 7

WOMEN: WILL SHE OR WON'T SHE?

"Sorry about your loss. On a brighter side, you could have
lost this one . . ."

—Fan mail snark

Women are evolution's greatest gift. They nurture, protect, and
educate their offspring, ensuring survival of the next generation. In
fact, female Darwin Award winners are incredibly rare! But they do
appear from time to time, and we've collected seven of these elusive
elegies here.

*Double Dip • She Talks Faster Than She Walks •
Wetting the Bed • Missed (but Not Missed By) the Bus •
A Clear Lesson • Epitaph—She Liked Feathers • Pill Pusher*

*For more female contenders, see:
Not Even Half-Baked, p. 17,
Christmas Light Zinger, p. 188,
and Medieval Mayhem, p. 238.*

Darwin Award Winner: Double Dip

Confirmed by Darwin

Featuring a woman, water, alcohol, and a moped

3 JUNE 2009, NORTH CAROLINA | Greensboro was inundated with four inches of pouring rain in two hours, stranding cars on flooded roads. Rosanne T., on her moped, was not deterred. She hopped on and drove to a convenience store where she "possibly had a beer," according to her mother, before deciding to blunder home through the storm.

> **"My moped has two rubber wheels, Mom, I'll be fine."**

North Carolina does not require a license to drive a moped.

Ms. T. had acquired hers two years previously after a DUI conviction.

The highway patrol had blocked off several roads that were flooded, including Rosanne's path home. But she rode right past the officer and the barriers, lost control of her vehicle, and fell into the swollen creek below. The officer retrieved rope from his vehicle and proceeded to haul her from the water, saving her from potential doom.

He then interviewed the woman, presumably inquiring about her motives for speeding through a police roadblock during a flash flood. When the officer returned to his patrol car to call in the incident, Rosanne took the opportunity to escape—*by jumping back into the creek!*

The officer attempted to rescue her again, but alas, it was too late.

The victim's mother speculated that her daughter's motivation for jumping into a flooded creek was to rescue her drowning moped. "She loved that thing."

Reference: news-record.com, Greensboro, NC, wxii12.com

Reader Comments

"Just because you have two rubber wheels does not mean you cannot drown . . ."

"North Carolina's finest . . . First-ever woman to become a finalist for the Darwin Awards."

"First woman *ever!!* Are we honored or what?! NOT!"

While North Carolina does not require a license to operate a moped, if a person is caught driving any vehicle (moped, golf cart, tractor, bicycle, etc.) on public roads while intoxicated, the state (and many states) will be able to prosecute for a DUI conviction.

Darwin Award Winner:
She Talks Faster Than She Walks

Confirmed by Darwin
Featuring a woman, car, and machismo

30 MAY 2009, LOUISIANA | Backseat drivers beware! Annoyed at how slowly her boyfriend was driving, Tamera B., twenty-two, encouraged him to pick up the pace so she could get to work on time. Joking that it would be faster to walk to work, she opened the door of the pickup truck and stuck her foot out—before falling out the open door to her death. Whoops!

But wait! Was her complaint valid?

Nope. Deputies of the jurisdictional sheriff's office stated that the truck was traveling at "highway speed" on I-12 at the time of the incident. Her death was ruled accidental.

Reference: New Orleans *Times-Picayune*, Nola.com

Reader Comment

"A small consolation—she got the last word!"

Darwin Award Winner: Wetting the Bed

Confirmed by Darwin

Featuring a woman, water, weather, and machismo!

27 OCTOBER 2009, ARKANSAS | Thirty-year-old Ms. Devan-LeAnn of Shongaloo, Louisiana, was visiting Lake Erling with a male friend. Recent bouts of heavy rain had resulted in a flood of runoff water, and the two decided it would be "fun" to take a mattress careening down the surging water in the spillway.

An air mattress would be one thing. Unfortunately Devan-LeAnn was riding a foam egg-crate mattress pad. Imagine a wet foam pad. Are you sinking yet?

According to her friend, Devan-LeAnn simply vanished from sight at dusk. The next morning her body was found in a tangle of trees seventy yards below the spillway.

Parents, warn your children! Wetting the bed can be deadly.

Reference: *Arkansas Democrat-Gazette, Texarkana Gazette*

Reader Comments

"LOL! I'm glad I'm over that habit [embarrassed laugh]."

"At least she died in bed . . ."

Darwin Award Winner:
Missed (but Not Missed By) the Bus

Confirmed by Darwin

Featuring a woman, a vehicle, and a can of pop!

13 AUGUST 2009, CANADA | A twenty-four-year-old was ironically successful in her attempt to catch a bus in Quebec City. Clutching a can of pop, the woman ran into a *restricted area* and tried to flag down a forty-five-foot bus that had left on time—a minute ago—without her. As she tried her best to get herself noticed, she herself failed to notice that the bus was making a swift turn in her direction.

A veteran driver pointed out that drivers cannot hear anything over the sound of their engines. The woman stood her ground—and disappeared beneath the turning bus. Suddenly, she was no longer able to concern herself with getting there on time.

Considering that you have to go out of your way to get mowed down by a bus in a transit center—such as sneaking around barricades into a restricted area and running under the tires—the bus company said it does not plan to increase security.

Instead of riding home in a crowded bus, the deceased woman enjoyed one last luxury: a private one-way trip "home" in a hearse.

Reference: *Le Journal de Quebec*, CBC.ca

At-Risk Survivor: A Clear Lesson

Unconfirmed Personal Account
Featuring women and a glass door

2009 | When she was younger, a college student had accidentally run right through the glass sliding doors at home. Ouch! After that painfully "clear" lesson, her family put decals on the doors to keep it from happening again. After all, glass is expensive.

Years later, the student was home for school break. She was doing some chores for her parents when she decided to clean the sliding glass doors. She took off the decals, put them aside, and began to polish the glass. Then the family dog sidetracked her. When the industrious daughter

Father to daughter: "And *this* is why we pay all that tuition?"

returned to the kitchen a few minutes later, she had already forgotten about those glass doors.

She saw her sister in the backyard, walked at a fast pace toward her, and smashed right through the glass again!

The lesson? Never—never—walk away from an unfinished job.

This lesson was learned all too dearly by the author herself (p. 3).

Reference: Anonymous

Darwin Award Winner:
Epitaph—She Liked Feathers

Confirmed by Darwin

Featuring a woman and gravity

22 FEBRUARY 2009, UK | A woman in her forties was following a coastal footpath along the top of a cliff in Devon. While enjoying the natural scenery she noticed a beautiful feather floating just out of reach. Fencing was in place to protect people from falling, but this protective fencing was no match for the allure of a feather blown by the breeze. While chasing the elusive plume, the woman climbed the fence, slipped, and fell.

An experiment much like this one was performed from the top of the leaning Tower of Pisa. There is truly a fine line between genius and madness. Our heroine was on the wrong side of that line.

Eighty vertical feet later, the experiment data point landed.

She was airlifted to the hospital, but unfortunately there was no cure for what ailed her, and she died of head injuries the following day.

Reference: Telegraph.co.uk

At-Risk Survivor: Pill Pusher

Confirmed by Reliable Eyewitness
Featuring a woman, teen, and medicine

Darwin says, "We asked for medical submissions and have greatly enjoyed the responses!"

PENNSYLVANIA | My husband worked at a small, busy rural pharmacy. His customers were hard-working, simple people. Early one morning he dispensed a prescription to the mother of a teenager for anti-nausea tablets and suppositories, labeled with what he *thought* were clear directions.

Early that evening he received a phone call from the child's mother, asking when the medications would take effect. Knowing that the suppository *should* have taken effect within an hour, he asked which form of the medicine she had given the child. The mother said she had tried both tablets and suppositories, but the patient was still experiencing severe nausea.

Since the child was evidently sicker than originally diagnosed, my husband told her that she needed to call the doctor and ask for further instructions. Then the mother asked the key question: *Should she have unwrapped the suppository before her child swallowed it?* That winner was quickly followed by her inquiry as to how far she should have inserted the tablet rectally, or rather should it have been inserted vaginally?

To this day, he includes directions for unwrapping suppositories before use, as well as stating that tablets should be taken by mouth!

Reference: Ann Boncal

Reader Comments

"Do we *really* need suppository instructions?"

"I used to think people had *some* brains."

". . . and they say a pharmacy is dull?"

SCIENCE INTERLUDE
SEX ON THE BRAIN

By Robert Adler

Suppose our big brains didn't evolve for practical reasons such as better hunting, gathering, or fighting—things that our less-endowed primate cousins do quite well. What if the explosive growth in brain power that made us what we are today had nothing to do with fitness, but everything to do with sex?

That's what evolutionary psychologist Geoffrey Miller thinks, and presents in convincing detail in his book, *The Mating Mind: How Sexual Choice Shaped the Evolution of Human Nature. (New York: Vintage, 2001)*

> What counted wasn't the ability to pitch a spear more accurately, but the ability to pitch a good pickup line.

Our brains ballooned over the last two million years not to make us more fit on the savannah, but to make us more marketable in the Pleistocene equivalent of pickup bars, Miller says. Sexual selection—the individual mating choices of thousands of generations of our ancestors—is driving the growth of our big brains.

Art, Music, Language, and Creativity

Sexual selection's fingerprints are all over a bouquet of complex and colorful human capacities, valued and attractive talents that have little to no survival value. Miller's list includes expressive arts such as music, poetry, painting, dance, personal decoration, and universally admired qualities—such as generosity and heroism—that are tough to explain based on survival of the fittest.

"Theories of human mental evolution just weren't accounting for (these) aspects of human behavior," says Miller. Sexual selection, which accounts for many of the most surprising features of plants and animals, does a much better job of explaining a range of useless human talents. His ideas may even shed light on the evolutionary history that lurks behind the fatal displays of risk-taking and derring-do that garner Darwin Awards.

Survival of the Sexiest

The idea started with Darwin. In *The Descent of Man, and Selection in Relation to Sex*, Darwin argued that evolution winnows every generation through two sieves: *fitness*, which selects adaptations that help us survive; and *sexiness* (sexual selection), which selects adaptations that help us mate. Fitness selection might lead to warm fur, and the ability to communicate. Sexual selection might lead to long hair and a pleasant voice.

Fitness selection has enjoyed extensive scientific scrutiny while sexual selection has been an afterthought, but current researchers are taking an avid interest in sex. After all, survival is worthless, from an evolutionary point of view, unless you manage to woo and win a mate.

Survival is worthless unless you manage to woo and win a mate.

Sexual selection is powered by two main engines: competition among potential suitors and individual choice of mate.

Competitive selection—competition for mating rights—sets up an arms race that leads to aggressive, well-armed males who fight for access to females. Picture a male lion and his pride, or a stag sporting his rutting rack of antlers. While competition leads to fairly predictable outcomes, mate selection is another matter.

Mate selection—evolution's wild card—is based on whatever aesthetic qualities happen to lead an individual to mate with one partner and reject another. Mate selection can home in on any feature or behavior that happens to attract and impress the opposite sex. Favorites include bright colors, rhythmic movements, and melodious voices, but there are practically as many possibilities as there are species.

Through a hypothetical process called *runaway sexual selection,* those attractive qualities can be exaggerated to an astonishing degree. You can see it coming—

Sexual selection is powered by competitive selection and mate selection.

the bird everyone agrees is frivolous—the peacock! Mate selection led to the insane plumage of peacocks, the meter-tall architectural nest of the bowerbird, and perhaps to many of humanity's most cherished creative abilities. The next time you show your moves on the dance floor, wink at the driver of that flashy sports car, or splurge on a new tattoo, thank your smart, sexy, selective ancestors—who knew there was more to life than mere survival.

Choosy Men Choose Too

One important way in which Miller departs from Darwin is in the kind of mate selection he sees operating in the human animal. Darwin's examples of mate selection involved flashy males showing off to attract choosy females. Miller points out that if that had been a dominant pattern in human evolution, men and women might have evolved minds as different as the plumage of peacocks and peahens.

Instead, human mental capacities seemingly evolved through mutual mate choice—our male and female forebears were *equally* attracted to smart, creative, communicative mates. Men have the reputation of being less picky than women when choosing sexual partners, but recent research has shown that that's not the case when it comes to serious relationships that lead to children.

Our brains are more like entertainment centers than Swiss army knives.

Let the Big-Brained Beware

However much we value our verbal, creative, and interpersonal skills, there's a catch. If Miller is right and our brains are more like multifunction entertainment centers than Swiss army knives, if we have been bred more to woo and win mates than simply to survive, then we may be a lot less practical and rational than we think.

Out of necessity, survival selects for realistic problem-solving minds, but sexual selection is not obliged to follow suit. It obviously favored human males who were driven to demonstrate their skills, even if that meant taking (*cough*) risks. Miller believes it also favored imaginative storytellers over plodding realists, creative dreamers and self-confident explorers over sensible worker bees.

It's encouraging to think that our minds evolved as much to dream, play, and create as to struggle to survive. "Our ancestors were more lovers than fighters," says Miller. "That's important for our self-concept as a species. It highlights the deep roots of love, and the attractiveness of moral virtues."

Still, we shouldn't be surprised if some of those playful dreamers "slide" off thousand-foot cliffs (see p. 227), do one pull-up too many on the ski-lift drive wheel (p. 51), or find other creative, dramatic and high-risk ways to take themselves and their genes over the edge and into the annals of the Darwin Awards.

REFERENCES:

Charles Darwin, *The Descent of Man, and Selection in Relation to Sex* (London: John Murray, 1871).

G. Gehrer and G. F. Miller, eds., *Mating Intelligence: Sex, Relationships, and the Mind's Reproductive System* (Mahwah, NJ: Lawrence Erlbaum, 2007).

G. F. Miller, *The Mating Mind: How Sexual Choice Shaped the Evolution of Human Nature* (New York: Vintage, 2001).

G. F. Miller, "Sexual selection for moral virtues," *Quarterly Review of Biology* 82(2) (2007), 97–125.

M. Ridley, *The Red Queen: Sex and the Evolution of Human Nature* (New York: Harper Perennial, 2003).

CHAPTER 6

THE FAST TRACK: TRAINS, CARS, AND BAR STOOLS!

"The Darwin Awards are always interesting. I sometimes
wish that certain people would try to win one . . . You
know who they are."

—excerpt from Fan mail

Vehicular misadventure is always a winning ticket. The following
tales offer variations on a theme with squished sports cars, military
men gone wild, dancing drivers, insurance fraud, and the invention
of a whole new type of hybrid. Hang on to your hats . . .

*Motorized Bar Stool • A One-Track Mind • Poor Decision on
a Major Scale • Painkiller • Mock Death • Chutes and Spills •
ICanSayIToldYouSo • Flying Door • Clap-Clap-Clap Your Hands
• Cats Land on All Fours*

At-Risk Survivor: Motorized Bar Stool

Confirmed by Darwin

Featuring vehicles, alcohol, and do-it-yourself innovation

4 MARCH 2009, NEW JERSEY | The Newark Fire Department was called to assist a man who had suffered injuries from a crash—while driving a motorized bar stool! The man claimed that his lawn-mower-bar-stool hybrid could reach a speedy thirty-eight mph on its five-horsepower engine, but he was traveling a sedate twenty mph when he rolled and crashed while making a turn.

Although under the speed limit, he was over the drink limit. During a police interview at the hospital, he admitted to consuming "about fifteen beers." When numbers reach the double digits, it's hard to be exact. The driver was issued a citation for operating a vehicle (classified as "all others") while intoxicated, and driving with a suspended license—presumably the motivation behind his motorized creation.

He pleaded not guilty—demanding, in fact, a jury trial before his peers. Those of you who drive motorized bar stools and other unconventional vehicles, watch your mailbox for a jury summons.

If the twenty-eight-year-old inventor wants to drive a hybrid, he should consider modifying his bar stool to corner better—once he regains the right to operate a motorized vehicle on public roads.

Reference: *Newark Advocate, The Boston Globe*

Reader Comments

"License to Spill."

"Hybrid vigor—or evolutionary dead end?"

"A motorized barstool will never be stable. He needs a wider wheelbase. Perhaps a motorized gurney?"

A TV news report featuring video of the motorized bar stool: www.DarwinAwards.com/book/barstool.html

Darwin Award Winner: A One-Track Mind

Confirmed by Darwin
Featuring train versus car!

16 JULY 2008, ITALY | Gerhard Z., sixty-eight, was queued at a traffic light in his Porsche Cayenne. Before one reaches the light, there is a railroad crossing, and Gerhard had not let the queue progress forward far enough **"Was he texting?"** before he drove onto the tracks. As you might imagine, given Murphy's Law, a train was coming. The safety bars came down, leaving the Porsche trapped.

According to witnesses, it took the driver a while to realize he was stuck on the rails.

Finally he jumped from the car and started to run—straight toward the oncoming train, waving his arms in an attempt to save his SUV! The attempt was partly successful, in that the car received less damage than its owner, who landed thirty meters away. Attempts to revive him were unsuccessful.

Actually, one is well advised to run toward the train, so that the collision throws the car in the opposite direction away from you. In that respect, the gentleman was in the right. The caveat is that you run toward the train *alongside* the tracks, not *on* the tracks!

The moral of the story? Momentum Always Wins.

Reference: *l'Adige* (Italian daily paper)

Reader Comments

"He needs better training."

"Man did that train pepper that Cayenne!"

"Cars are easier to replace than internal organs."

"A dark and twisted example of momentum and transfer of energy."

Wendy was traveling in Egypt. At night, on busy roads, the car headlights were so dim they were almost useless. It seemed so dangerous! Why were the headlights "browned out"? . . . A local guide said, "We dim the headlights to make the bulbs last longer." The bulbs last longer, but what about the occupants? Madness!

"Crazy as carrying timber into the woods."

—Roman idiom

Darwin Award Winner:
Poor Decision on a Major Scale

Confirmed by Reliable Eyewitness
Featuring a military vehicle and a bed!

SEPTEMBER 1997, FORT POLK, LOUISIANA | The 82nd Airborne Division was on its periodic training junket to Fort Polk. One of the many items stressed at briefings before a training mission of this proportion is the fact that there are many untrained people running about the area, at all times of day and night, in all kinds of vehicles, most of them large.

During the training we were reminded, when sleeping in the woods at night, *be sure to sleep at the base of a large tree.* Drivers may or may not be wearing night vision equipment, and may or may not be familiar with the roads, but even the most misguided driver will avoid a large tree, thus assuring your own safety.

Sleep by a tree, and you will wake up in the morning.

This reminder was repeated in light of recent events.

An army major had been assigned to the 82nd Airborne Division as an observer controller. One night he decided to bed down on what he deemed to be an unused old trail. Down the "unused" trail later that night a random driver drove, perhaps taking a wrong turn in the darkness, or perhaps taking a shortcut from point A to point B. Somehow this driver found himself on a road with a few "disconcerting bumps" but he continued to drive on.

When the young private assigned as the major's

radio operator roused himself from sleep (safely at the base of a large tree a short distance from the trail) he quickly discovered the lifeless body of his charge. One poor decision took the life of the major—a man with a college degree, a commission from Congress, and years of responsibilities that *included* reminding trainees to sleep away from the roads.

He was pronounced DRT (Dead Right There).

Reference: Galen Fisher, B Co. 3/325

Reader Comments

"Superior officer? I don't think so!"

"What happened to the sergeant who was assigned to keep the major out of trouble?"

"And to think, I wanted to be promoted to Major!"

"That was certainly a major catastrophe."

Darwin Award Winner: Painkiller

Confirmed by Darwin
Featuring cars, drugs, and insurance

17 OCTOBER 2009, MINNESOTA | On October 26, charges were dismissed against Lucas William Stenning, thirty-two, who six weeks earlier had pleaded guilty to knowingly violating registration required of a predatory offender. Charges were dismissed . . . because Lucas was dead.

In a related story, on the afternoon of October 17 in the city of Bock, an injured "hit-and-run victim" was reported. The pedestrian, found on the side of the road, died in the ambulance at the scene.

In a related story, police reported that a thirty-two-year-old man had concocted a scheme to *stage an accident* in order to obtain prescription drugs. The plan was to jump out of a moving vehicle, become injured, go to the hospital, and receive narcotic painkillers. ("Dude, that's brilliant!") That plan failed when its mastermind, Lucas William Stenning, died at the scene due to head injuries.

In other words, Lucas avoided a serious legal problem because he was deceased due to injuries he caused himself by leaping from a moving vehicle in order to obtain prescription painkillers. Ouch!

Reference: *Mille Lacs Messenger, Mille Lacs County Times*

Reader Comments

"Some people just don't realize there *is* such a thing as going too far."

"I guess 'no warrant needed' on this one."

"Sounds like one of our Lil' Darlins'."

Darwin Award Winner: Mock Death

Confirmed by Darwin
Featuring a vehicle and insurance

1 NOVEMBER 2009, BELGIUM | Police received a desperate call from a man who had been attacked on a motorway near the town of Liege. When the policemen arrived, they found Thierry B., thirty-seven, lying dead on the ground, his body stabbed, his car burning. Witnesses had seen a big truck driving away.

But there was no evidence of fighting or struggling around the body—only the knife wounds on his shoulder and neck. Puzzled, inspectors analyzed Thierry's cell phone calls. He had recently reconnected with an old friend, a fact that intrigued Inspector Clouseau. I mean, Commissioner Lamoque. Childhood friend, lost sight of for ten years, back in touch? Lamoque invited the forty-two-year-old friend in for a chat about the roadside aggression.

Turns out, Thierry was aggrieved regarding insurance money he felt he was owed but was never paid, after his restaurant burned two years before. He had asked his old friend to bring him a knife and a jerrican of fuel, and leave him alone on the motorway: a man with a plan to get the insurance money one way or another.

The "victim" then set his car on fire, called the police, and stabbed himself, accidentally cutting an artery in his own neck. By the time his simulated act of violence was over, he was over too, face against the ground ten yards from his burned car. Roll credits on this little drama.

Reference: *La Dernière Heure* (Belgium)

Reader Comments

"Mock aggression mocks death."

"Faking it."

"They'll probably raise his rates."

"Objection! How do we know this was not murder or suicide by persons unknown? L. Ron Hubbard, anyone?"—Conspiracy theorist

At-Risk Survivor: Chutes and Spills

Unconfirmed Military Account, Suspected Urban Legend
Featuring the military, parachutes, vehicles, and plenty of machismo

2003, IRAQ | A group of marines obtained some surplus para-chutes that had been taken out of circulation. The silk chutes were good for nothing more than providing shade in Iraq—or midsummer mischief. To begin with, the marines popped two chutes and competed to see who could run one hundred meters fastest while dragging a chute, but in short order they moved on to more daring adventures.

The most prominent idea floated was either to jump off the top of the barracks or paraglide from a truck driven along the beach. Obviously jumping off a building wasn't wise, and the long drive to the beach precluded immediate gratification. But why not deploy a canopy, like a drag-racing parachute, behind a car while driving?

With proper planning, this might have caused no more damage than a missing bumper, but without proper planning it almost provided one lance corporal with a premature death. You see, in the interest of *saving time,* the marines attached the chute to the driver instead of the car. He buckled in, and the chute was tossed out of the sunroof of the Eclipse.

The first two runs were a "failure" because the chute didn't catch enough air. After a brief reconnoiter the men held the chute open behind the Eclipse while the driver, now pumped full of adrenaline, revved the engine and popped the clutch. The stretch of road was no longer than two hundred yards, but it was the longest drive ever taken by that marine.

The canopy quickly expanded to its fullest, the loose cords pulled taut, and the driver was lifted dramatically off his seat. He found himself suspended in the cabin with only the seat belt preventing him from being yanked through the sunroof. What with being pulled in different directions, the cord lacerations, and the fear of crashing into barriers dead ahead, he had had enough. However, in his position against the roof of the cab, he couldn't do much about the situation. The young man realized that he had a legit chance of being the next dumb marine to win a Darwin Award.

After what seemed like an eternity, he managed to stretch his limbs far enough to depress the clutch and pull the emergency brake. The car stopped suddenly—not to the sound of screeching tires, but to the sound of cracking fiberglass. More on that in a moment.

With the car at rest, the marine expected to slide down to his seat and beat a hasty retreat from that death trap. Instead he remained inexplicably pressed against the roof. He struggled with the seat belt, released the five-point parachute harness, and finally slithered out of the car, breathing a prayer of gratitude.

The small crowd rippled with the nervous laughter of people who had narrowly survived a runaway roller coaster. Observers had seen the parachute sway violently from side to side behind the small car. At the very instant the driver had pulled the brake, the chute had caught on a concrete Jersey barrier next to the buildings.

It was a gut-wrenching moment. If he had braked a second later, the marine would have been crushed between the opposing forces of the moving vehicle and the stationary parachute. The loud cracking fiberglass noise? That was the sound of the cords compressing the sunroof and breaking the spoiler loose from the trunk.

A sailor who witnessed the stunt from the E-club came running out with an expression of disbelief. "Are you trying to get a Darwin Award, marine? *Why* did you do that?"

The marine answered, in the most matter-of-fact voice, "We got bored."

> **"The *greatest* fighting force in the world, but maybe not the *smartest*."**

Reference: Anonymous

TRUE OR FICTITIOUS?

Readers are skeptical of this scenario. They argue that if he was pinned to the roof of the car and could barely reach the clutch, then obviously his foot was off the accelerator and engine braking would have brought a standard shift vehicle to a rapid halt. Furthermore, they point out that the U.S. Marines and other branches of the military are not allowed to have personal vehicles in a war zone. It would have had to have been a military grade vehicle, not an Eclipse. There certainly are several glaring inconsistencies!

WHAT DO YOU THINK?
www.DarwinAwards.com/book/chute

At-Risk Survivor: ICanSayIToldYouSo

Confirmed by Reliable Eyewitness
Featuring medicine, vehicles, and machismo

JULY 2009, IOWA | A doctor at the University of Iowa's oral sur-
gery clinic relayed the almost unbelievable story of a patient he had
treated in the emergency room. As you will soon find out, it took a
medical miracle to prevent this man from taking home the grand
prize.

The man, in his late twenties, and his wife were driving down
the highway when they were involved in a one-car accident from
which the wife emerged unscathed, while her husband sustained
two broken legs, multiple rib fractures, a broken arm, a broken col-
larbone, and the worst facial trauma the fifty-five-year-old oral sur-
geon had ever seen. "We put his forehead back together like a
puzzle, intermixing pieces of bone and metal plates."

Wondering how there could be such a fantastic difference in
their injuries, Doctor decided to ask Wife a few questions.

She said that the couple had been arguing about the man's reckless habits, specifically his love for "street skating."

In an activity almost too absurd to exist, the participants get a
vehicle going at a good speed, sometimes up to thirty mph, open
the door, hang on for dear life, and drag the soles of their feet on the
pavement.

The wife began the discussion in the car that day by using her
sane mind to tell her Evel Knievel–wannabe husband that he was
going to get killed by willingly jumping out of, hanging onto, and

dragging his feet alongside a moving vehicle. Nettled, Husband set out to prove to Wife that this activity was, in fact, not dangerous.

Traveling at sixty mph—in a car he himself was driving—he opened the door, got a good grip, and hopped out, forgetting that he was traveling at double or triple the "normal" speed for this asinine stunt. His feet immediately caught the pavement and were pulled out from under him, but he did not fall from the car quite yet. He held on long enough for the out-of-control vehicle to roll into a ditch and for him to come into face-first contact with a telephone pole, stopping the argument faster than an auctioneer could spit out, "ICanSayIToldYouSo."

Miraculously this champ will live to fight another day with a fully functional—or at least as functional as it was prior to the accident—brain, as he sustained no lasting head injury.

Reference: Anonymous

The next story features this guy's identical twin . . .

At-Risk Survivor: Flying Door

Unconfirmed Military Account
Featuring the military, a vehicle, and machismo

1973, VIRGINIA | When I was in the Marines, a bottom-enlisted and an NCO were required to stand twenty-four-hour watch together. One evening I showed up for duty to find the NCO, whom we'll call Todd, limping and covered with dozens of fresh scabs! He was reluctant to reveal what caused his injuries until I promised not to tell. I lived with that promise for thirty years, until now.

This NCO Todd had an NCO friend whom we'll call Dutch, and these guys would do just about anything for a laugh. The two NCOs ended up working together in the squadron truck and had an idea good for a few laughs.

Dutch was possessed of great upper body strength; he had been a Greco-Roman wrestler in high school and was still an active weight lifter. Dutch would put his elbow outside the open window, hang on to the door under his armpit, and when Todd made a left turn Dutch would open the door and swing out with the centrifugal force of the turn, riding on the door under his arm. Good fun, huh?

These two were having a few laughs with their flying door routine, all well and good, until one turn brought the open door too close to a fire hydrant. The hydrant caught the bottom corner of the door and the door rebounded, slamming shut at over thirty miles an hour and sending Dutch sailing across the vinyl bench seat and slamming into Todd with enough force to knock open the driver's door and eject him from the vehicle!

Dutch managed to recover the wheel and prevent Todd from being run down. Both men were in pain for weeks, and this being the military, both spent long hours in extra duty. After all, they were guilty of risking U.S. government property.

Reference: Carin Gleason

MAD SCIENCE: PROJECT STEVE

Creationists try to convince the public that evolution is a "theory in crisis" by compiling lists of scientists who doubt evolution. The National Center for Science Education responded with Project Steve.[*] Instead of compiling a list of ten thousand scientists who support evolution, they decided to poke fun at the nuts by compiling a list of only those scientists named "Steve" who affirm the validity of evolution. Steve was chosen in honor of the late Stephen Jay Gould, beloved evolutionary biologist. In March 2010 there were 1,138 Steves on the list! Because Steves comprise only about 1 percent of scientists, Project Steve makes the point that **scientists support evolution.**

---

[*] National Center for Science Education, "The List of Steves," http://ncse.com/taking-action/list-steves.

At-Risk Survivor:
Clap-Clap-Clap Your Hands

Unconfirmed Personal Account
Featuring a vehicle and music!

NOVEMBER 2009, POUGHKEEPSIE, NEW YORK | "I was driving down the road when the car in front of me suddenly accelerated, then stopped accelerating but continued going straight as the road curved, ultimately crashing into a rail. I pulled over to help, and asked the driver what caused the crash. He told me that 'The Cha Cha Slide' was playing on the radio and he was dancing along. When the lyrics came to 'Left foot, left stomp,' he did just that, flooring the accelerator. Then the lyrics commanded, 'Freeze,' and he froze, and then, 'Everybody, clap your hands'—at which point he crashed."

Reference: Anonymous

Reader Comments

"I told you that dancing was evil!"

"A nearly fatal case of the clap."

At-Risk Survivor: Cats Land on All Fours

Unconfirmed

Featuring work, vehicles, and gravity

8 MAY 2008, CALIFORNIA | Twenty-four-year-old Andrew, an operator for a gravel company, did not intend to perform a death-defying stunt with a forty-ton construction machine. He was only trying to free a bulldozer stuck atop a fifty-foot-high pile of dirt that it had been pushing. Despite several better options, Andrew decided to pull the stuck machine backward with an old front-end Caterpillar loader.

Driving up a dirt ramp at a forty-degree angle is nerve-racking enough without doing so knowing that your vehicle's brakes are inoperable and in need of repair. The operator in question knew that when he decided to use the machine to free the 'dozer, something he should not have been doing with *any* loader under *any* circumstance. To compound the risk, Andrew decided to improve traction by loading the Caterpillar's bucket with dirt to give it more weight.

At the top of the hill, Andrew did as he was trained: He took his foot off the throttle and hit the button to engage the parking brake—forgetting that, on CAT loaders, setting the parking brake automatically puts the transmission in neutral. He unfastened his seat belt and began to exit the loader, which was imperceptibly rolling backward.

When Andrew noticed, he jumped back into the

cab and hit the brake pedal, but nothing happened. The loader continued downhill.

Beyond the edge of the property was a steep drop down to the next property. A five-foot dirt berm protected the edge so trucks would not accidentally drive off the cliff. At twenty-five mph, this berm did little to slow forty tons of rolling steel and dirt, but it did give the loader a good launching height. In a stunt that would make Evel Knievel sweat, the machine careened up the berm and launched into the air, clearing the cliff and landing on the adjacent property thirty-five feet below and fifty feet away.

Andrew was thrown through the rear windshield and onto the engine compartment. Miraculously the loader landed on all four tires, and he was able to walk away with just a few cuts and bruises. Looking back at the incident, Andrew laughs and says he proved that *a CAT always lands on all fours.*

Reference: Pending OSHA Report

SCIENCE INTERLUDE
LEFT BEHIND: VESTIGIAL STRUCTURES

By Stephanie Pappas

The human appendix is as active as a drowned worm. Just three or four inches long, this dead-end tube dangles off the large intestine in the lower right side of the abdomen. If you were born without one, you will likely never know. Surgically remove it, and you'll carry on eating and excreting without a hitch. Charles Darwin himself declared the thing "useless."

Vestigial structures—body parts that have lost their original function but linger on in a rudimentary form—are everywhere. One species diverges from another and no longer needs those pesky gills, extra teeth, or that third eyelid, but the developmental pathways that build those structures soldier on. Unless the vestigial bits and pieces actively harm an organism's chances for procreation, they simply stick around.

> **Charles Darwin himself declared the appendix "useless."**

Whale Legs, Pili, and Pinnae

Vestigiality explains weird stuff like whales with leg bones under their blubber, and blind cave fish that form embryonic eyes only to have those eyes collapse and vanish before the fish hatch. We humans experience the effects of evolutionary leftovers every time we feel the prickle of gooseflesh. When we're cold or scared, tiny *erector pili* muscles at the base of each hair follicle snap to attention, and—*BAM*—goose bumps. It's a nice reflex if you're a German Shepherd, but doesn't do much for *Homo sapiens*.

The *erector pili* is not the only body part whose heyday has passed. Certain small muscles in our forearms and feet are vestigial remnants of larger muscles that helped our ancestors swing on branches. Wisdom teeth are a reminder of a time when jaws were larger and teeth more likely to need replacing. Muscles around our ears helped a long-ago ancestor swivel the organs toward faint sounds, but today they're useful only for the occasional ear-wiggling party trick.

Ear muscles are today useful only for party tricks.

Peer Into the Past

While vestigial structures are a fine tool for evolutionary biologists trying to tease out the connections between species, if you *really* want to understand our ancestry, it's best to peer into the genome itself.

As it turns out, that genome is a messy place full of evolutionary leftovers.

Our DNA is a hodgepodge of mutations, recombinations, and

genetic cut-and-paste. Among the remnants of this process are *pseudogenes,* which resemble functional genes but don't code for proteins the way functional genes should. Some pseudogenes are broken pieces of genes that have since vanished—no functional versions are found. Other pseudogenes are old copies of genes that have evolved into newer, functional versions. These "backup copies" are a snapshot of what once was.

Pseudogenes are fossils of old DNA that show us what once was.

Pseudogenes are a *big* chunk of our genome: We have an estimated 25,000 protein-coding genes and 20,000 pseudogenes. Pseudogenes are almost as common as genes!

Pseudogenes and the Blight of Scurvy

Pseudogenes provide a fossil record of how the modern genome came to be. Here's an example:

Most animals make their own vitamin C. Humans cannot. We have to eat vitamin C–rich food or suffer the blight of scurvy.

Scientists traced this human disease to *a single pseudogene,* the broken remains of a gene that once enabled our ancestors to synthesize vitamin C. Pretty neat, huh? They found the fossil remains of the very gene that enabled our furry forefathers to synthesize vitamin C. The gene stopped working approximately 40 million years ago; since then its pseudogene fossil has been perched on chromosome 8, quietly accumulating random mutations.

At the time we lost the vitamin C gene, any individual that avoided vitamin C–rich foods such as citrus would die. That's what happens when natural selection is operating on a species: A large number of people

without the necessary gene or attribute die before they can reproduce. All surviving animals were genetically wired (and perhaps
culturally inclined) to eat juicy oranges and pineapple and toma-
toes and so forth.

Retired Pseudogene Caught Working

It's not easy to be sure that a gene is inactive. Some so-called pseudogenes are actually pretty busy. Research in pond snails and mice
shows that some stretches of DNA formerly labeled pseudogenes
are actually transcribed into RNA that regulates their protein coun-
terparts. One of these was discovered accidentally in the course of
genetically engineering lab mice.

Researchers inserted a gene sequence into a mouse pseudogene
(*Makorin1-p1*) intended as a control—a blank—nothing should happen. But to the scientists' surprise, the resulting babies died, for the
most part. The few survivors displayed terrible deformities: Bones
cells were laid out wrong, leading to weak and brittle skeletons.
Multiple cysts grew on their kidneys and livers. And they had skin
defects—for instance, the epithelium that covers the embryos' eyes
didn't form properly, so their eyes were open in the womb.

Why was the disruption of the pseudogene so catastrophic?

Recall that a gene is a sequence of DNA, and its DNA is transcribed into many RNA copies, which are templates for building
a protein. Knocking out the pseudogene is catastrophic, the researcher hypothesized, because the pseudogene is still being
transcribed into RNA but the cell does not use it to build a protein.
Instead, the pseudogene RNA seems to stabilize the transcription

of the nearby working gene (aptly named *Makorin1*). Knocking out the *stabilizing* pseudogene impairs the mouse's ability to make the *Makorin1* protein.

Darwin himself noted that a vestigial structure could be useless for its primary anatomical function, but retain a secondary anatomical role. *Makorin1-p1* is the broken remnant of a once-functional gene, but it is not a dead fossil. It now acts as a regulator of its more evolved offspring, *Makorin1*. In both mice and primates, other "pseudogenes" have been caught making RNA, and presumably some of them have similar regulatory effects.

> "Rudimentary for one, even the more important . . . perfectly efficient for the other."
> —Darwin

Worn Out or Working?

The debate over what structures are actually vestigial is not new. In fact, Darwin theorized on a dozen human vestigialities, including muscles of the ear, wisdom teeth, the appendix, the tail bone, body hair, and the semilunar fold in the corner of the eye in *The Descent of Man, 1871*.

Twenty-two years later, anatomist Robert Wiedersheim counted 83 vestigial structures, a figure that swelled to 180 during sworn testimony at the 1925 Scopes Monkey Trial. Vestigial structures are literally "evidence" of evolution! Some of the structures on that list are still considered vestigial, like our ear wigglers. Others, like the pituitary gland, have turned out to be very useful indeed, at least if you like your endocrine system in working condition.

Evidence of a use for something once considered worthless is always cause for excitement, even celebration, in laboratories. Remember the appendix, poster child for vestigial structures? True, it no longer does the tasks that a herbivore's appendix tackles. In koalas, for example, the organ is enormous and helps digest fibrous plant matter. But the fleshy tube may have a secondary use* as a holding pen for beneficial bacteria. The walls of the human appendix are coated in bacterial biofilms, and when sanitation is poor, the appendix can store and protect these good bacteria through bouts of diarrhea.

> The benefits of an appendix that stores good bacteria may be merely a happy side effect of an otherwise vestigial organ.

If the appendix, or a pseudogene, or even those silly ear-wiggling muscles turn out to be more useful than we suspected, it won't be an unprecedented discovery. Perhaps the leg bones of whales now serve as diving ballast. After all, evolution recycles. The broken bodies of former genes are ripe for reuse, and obsolete organs can be molded for new work.

As we dig deeper into answering *"What does that thing do?"* we uncover not only new questions, but also elegant new chains linking us to our evolutionary heritage.

---

* Pause for a moment to consider what else koalas might be doing with their *enormous fleshy tube*s . . .

CHAPTER 5

EXPLOSIONS: TICKING TIME BOMB

"Viva la muerte!"

Boom! Bang! Whoosh . . . ! Boys love toys that go *boom*, and true to form, we present myriad tales of bomb botches, dynamite disasters, carbide calamities, tobacco tragedies, and fuel fiascos. By some fluke, many explosions were not eternal rest bringers . . . this time!

Payback • Dynamite Rancher • Carbidschieten • A Really Bad Commute • Anchors Away! • Killer Fuel Economy • Mortar Fire • A Cushioned Blow • Homemade Howitzer • Nitrating the Unknown • Against the Odds • Caps'n'Hammer Kid • The Mettle of the Kettle • Boom Boom Bees

Darwin Award Winner: Payback

Confirmed by Darwin

Featuring criminals, money, and an explosion

> *"Neither a borrower nor a lender be; for loan oft loses both itself and Friend."*
>
> —*Polonius, in* Hamlet

27 DECEMBER 2008, SERBIA | Wanted in Croatia for murder and robbery of a post office, twenty-three-year-old Strahinja R. had good reason to leave the country. Fortunately for him, even bad guys have good friends. Aided and abetted by a friend who lent him 15,000 euros, Strahinja jumped the border and fled to Serbia, successfully evading prosecution.

Some loans can never be repaid. This was such a loan. Finding himself unable to earn or steal the funds needed to reimburse his benefactor, Strahinja attempted to end the matter in another way—by murdering him.

He crawled under his "friend's" Jeep to plant a powerful Repayment-brand explosive. However, the muffler was still hot, and the heat set off the bomb while Strahinja was beneath the vehicle. He died in the hospital in the capital city of Belgrade, vividly illustrating the truth of Shakespeare's warning, "Neither a borrower nor a lender be."

Even bad guys have good friends.

Reference: SETimes.com, eupm.org, tportal.hr

Darwin Award Winner: Dynamite Rancher

Confirmed by Darwin

Gun + dynamite = explosion

8 MAY 2009, UTAH | Fifty-nine-year-old Brent L. found a suspicious stash of dynamite in a shed on his five-thousand-acre ranch, located three miles south of the ATK Thiokol testing area where booster rockets for the space shuttle are designed. Details about this stash are scarce. Did it belong on the ranch? Was it hidden by thieves? Is it coincidence that the ranch is close to ATK Thiokol Ground Zero? Chief Deputy Potter said, "Whether the dynamite was his or whatever, that's yet to be determined."

Whatever its origins, the rancher was alarmed. He had good reason to worry. Old dynamite starts to sweat *nitroglycerine,* and once it starts it is unstable and can pop anytime. This well-known fact was surely known by the rancher. Fortunately the dynamite was not an old, sweating pile of unstableness. This stash of flash was something he felt he could deal with on his own.

> **"This stash of flash was something he could deal with on his own."**

Concerned for his family's safety—but his own, not so much—the rancher removed the dynamite from the shed, placed it in a field of knee-high grass, grabbed his shotgun, and backed away about forty yards. One would like to think that he stopped to consider his next action, but the evidence suggests otherwise. He aimed and fired. Guess what?

The dynamite exploded! Shrapnel hit the rancher squarely in

the head. The man was airlifted to the hospital, where he passed away.

Oddly enough, the Box County Sheriff's office refused to confirm the circumstances, saying they were "still looking into it" and the dynamite exploded "for some reason." But the first medical teams on the scene reported that the man shot the dynamite from forty yards. And, frankly, a man oughtn'ta.

Reference: Ogden *Standard-Examiner, Deseret News,*
The Tremonton Leader, standard.net

Reader Comment

"What gets into a guy's head to make him shoot at a high explosive . . . I guess the answer is shrapnel."

Darwin Award Winner: *Carbidschieten*

Confirmed by Darwin

Featuring holiday explosions

1 JANUARY 2010, THE NETHERLANDS | Every now and then a completely new window into the world opens before our eyes. Here we have rural Dutch families enjoying their traditional winter sport, *carbidschieten*, or carbide shooting. This diversion involves a ridiculously dangerous machine akin to a potato gun, designed to hurl projectiles from the mouth of a metal milk can.

Carbide shooting, that wacky Dutch New Year's celebration, begins with moistening calcium carbide (Ca_2C) and placing it in a large milk container. The damp Ca_2C emits acetylene (C_2H_2) gas that builds up inside the closed container. Then a spark is supplied, causing the pressurized gas bomb to *blow the lid* (or packing) off the milk jug.

Our nominee, a fifty-four-year-old male, was having the time of his life—right up until the moment he poured a container filled with *liquid oxygen* over a fire to "flare it up." The container obligingly exploded. He cashed in his chips, having ended with a flair.

Reference: www.nu.nl

Reader Comment

"Proof that Dutch should stick with gasification instead of trying oxyfuel."

At-Risk Survivor: A Really Bad Commute

Confirmed by Darwin

Featuring an explosion, work, and do-it-yourself

AUGUST 2008, THE NETHERLANDS | A thirty-three-year-old man was carpooling to work in Hindeloopen when he mentioned to his colleagues that he was carrying a self-made bomb. The driver immediately stopped the car and ejected the lunatic.

Outside the car, the lunatic—er, bomb maker—tried to disarm the device in an attempt to wheedle his way back into the vehicle. There was nothing to fear, everything was perfectly safe . . . until the bomb builder crossed the detonator wires. The dastardly device exploded, blasting away several of his nonvital body parts.

Police describe the hapless carpool driver as "shaken but unharmed." The bomber could be described as "shaken and unarmed."

Reference: spitsnieuws.nl

Reader Comments

"Disarmed."

"The malice of inanimate objects!"

"That was a really bad commute!"

At-Risk Survivor: Anchors Aweigh!

Unconfirmed

AUGUST 2006, KARELIA, RUS-SIA | Shiver me timbers! A man from Logmozero, a village located on a lake of the same name in northwestern Russia, was brought to the attention of police when concerned neighbors realized he was using a World War II aviation bomb as an anchor for his boat. Bomb experts said the twenty-five-kilogram curiosity was in working order and easily could have been triggered by an incautious action—such as weighing anchor—sending shrapnel flying five hundred meters from the epicenter. The detonator was missing and a metal hook had been *hammered into the device* by the owner, so that he could attach an anchor chain to it!

Darwin says, "Considered semi-confirmed because the media source is a website, 'Only in Russia,' about the strange things Russians do. A web search found no other sources. Additional confirmation is sought."

A metal hook had been hammered into the WWII device.

Reference: englishrussia.com

Merits Discussion: Killer Fuel Economy

Confirmed—But Is It a Darwin Award?

Featuring explosions, cars, and do-it-yourself innovation

7 NOVEMBER 2008, MALAYSIA | In the town of Batu Berendam, in the state of Malacca, Mohd H. was killed by an explosion at a petrol station while filling his van's tank with compressed natural gas. What made the normally routine process of fueling a vehicle go so badly wrong?

The answer begins with another kind of fuel: cooking gas.

In most Malaysian households, liquid petroleum gas (LPG) is purchased in tanks for use in the kitchen, instead of being drawn from a pipeline to the house as is common in America. The problem was that the man had converted his van to use cleaner-burning compressed natural gas (CNG) by hooking up an LPG *cooking gas tank,* rather than having the vehicle properly converted.

LPG tanks and CNG tanks are very different. LPG is a liquid while CNG is a compressed gas. CNG tanks must be able to contain one hundred times more pressure than LPG tanks.

Mohd's desire to economize on fuel was driven by practical reasons. The self-employed electrician ran a family business involving the repair and resale of secondhand electrical appliances. This business required frequent travels to Singapore and Johor, and much would be saved by converting the van to use a more economical fuel. Since twenty-five-year-old Mohd was knowledgeable about machinery, he decided to do it himself.

Somehow, the electrician managed to drain the fuel, remove the old tank, and weld a new tank into place without incident. No doubt pleased by his handiwork, he filled the tank with gas and turned the key. . . .

The LPG tank had been installed beneath the driver's seat, and the ignition system triggered an explosion that shattered the front portion of the vehicle and blew out two of its doors, killing the un-witting creator of the car bomb.

Reference: *The Malaysian Insider*

DARWIN SAYS, MERITS DEBATED!

We are divided about whether to give this man a Darwin Award. Local news reports indicate that inept do-it-yourself vehicle conversions are a national problem fueled by a *lack of knowledge* about combustion differences between CNG and LPG. On the other hand, this skilled electrician was *handy with tools* and knowledgeable about machines. Was he the engineer of his own demise, or simply a victim of circumstance?

An ancillary question is, how did he manage to drive the vehicle to the petrol station?

At-Risk Survivor: Mortar Fire

Unconfirmed Personal Account
Featuring acetylene gas and a can of Coke

2009 | This moment of blissfully pure and unadulterated stupidity happened while I was managing a successful franchise exhaust shop a few years back. I had won a contract to build custom exhausts on a series of hot rods. Due to the exacting workmanship required, I did these jobs after hours when I wasn't distracted by customers and staff.

Tired and a bit bored one evening, I took a break, swigged some soda, and set the Coke can down on the pipe rack. It fell neatly into a length of exhaust pipe. This raised some intriguing possibilities. I wondered if a small acetylene explosion would launch a can from the pipe. As it happened, an acetylene set was ready to hand, and I proceeded unimpeded with my experiment.

I welded a plate over one end of the tube, and bored a small hole in the side, just above the plate. I dropped an empty can down the pipe and introduced some acetylene and oxygen

> **I proceeded unimpeded with my experiment.**

though the hole. Test #1 went well. My trusty Zippo ignited the gas and there was a loud pop—but the can launched a measly ten feet in the air.

Being a perfectionist, I knew I could do better. The empty can was slightly smaller than the three-inch pipe, and much could be gained by wrapping the can to fit the pipe. Test #2 was better. The pop was louder, and the can launched upward with enough force to dent the tin roof of the building.

At this point I realized that I could do some damage, so I moved my enterprise out back behind the shop before proceeding with Test #3. I carefully wrapped a full Coke can with a rag, oiled to reduce friction. I rammed it hard down the pipe, but could only get it down about one foot. I aimed the tube straight up (to maximize altitude) and filled the three remaining feet with oxygen and acetylene. I must confess that I experienced a brief flash of doubt, but I overcame it, knelt down a careful eighteen inches from the pipe, and lit the mortar.

The result was considerably more violent than the prior launches.

I experienced a brief flash of doubt, but overcame it.

An extremely loud explosion and a searing flash of heat knocked me over. I caught a brief glimpse of a burning projectile disappearing at high velocity into the night sky. The recoil of the launch had driven the tube a foot into the ground, and the open end of the pipe sported a distinct bell shape. Luckily the pipe had held, and had not blown up in my face. Stunned, I staggered back into the shop and knocked over a six-foot length of exhaust pipe. Instead of the usual crash, I heard nothing but a high-pitched buzzing.

Break time was over! I carried on working.

Half an hour later I was surprised by two cops tapping me on the shoulder. They were a wee bit agitated, as they had been addressing me for a while and thought I was ignoring them. After much shouting and several written messages, it became apparent that they were investigating a loud explosion heard behind the twenty-thousand-liter propane tank at the gas station next door. The tank was ten feet away from my test site, behind a wooden fence!

The burning projectile disappeared into the night sky.

The gas station had, of course, been evacuated. Due to my impaired hearing, I had failed to notice the four fire engines outside and was blissfully unaware of the mayhem going on next door. Naturally enough, I denied any knowledge, but my burned and deaf state didn't help my case. Then a curious cop followed the oxy-acetylene hoses outside . . .

The incident cost me a severe telling-off by the cops and permanent hearing issues, but I count myself lucky. I must confess, though, sometimes I sit back and wonder . . . What was I thinking?

And where did that Coke can end up?

Reference: Anonymous

<u>Reader Comments</u>

"Admit it, the thought would cross *your* mind, too."

"Still working on that spud gun. Just upping the ante . . ."

"Remember acetylene + oxygen in balloons?"

At-Risk Survivor: A Cushioned Blow

Confirmed by Darwin

Featuring aerosol, an explosion, and cigarettes

CIGARETTES

Smoking destroys more than lung cells . . . if you try hard enough. Darwin's archive includes dozens of mishaps, from solo smokers wrapped in gauze (a mummy costume; a medical treatment) to military groups smoking near munitions (in the Philippines; in the Ukraine), from shooting yourself with butts to falling from a bus while sneaking a fag, there are *too many ways* cigarettes can hurt you. Please do whatever it takes to give up this dangerous habit.

13 OCTOBER 2008, GERMANY
One evening, a forty-two-year-old man fixed his punctured air mattress with a tire repair spray that, like all solvent-based aerosols, is flammable. Furthermore, he repaired the puncture while keeping the windows in his loft apartment tightly closed. The next morning, this airhead lit a smoke just before he opened the valve to deflate the air mattress. The resulting explosion wrecked most of the furnishings, part of the roof, and blew a window from the wall. The damage was so severe that a structural engineer condemned the flat! Narrowly missing a full-blown Darwin Award, our hero was taken to a burn-care unit and managed to recover from the brutal "attack" by his mattress.

Reference: presseportal.de

Another unsatisfactory mattress is featured in Wetting the Bed, p. 101.

At-Risk Survivor: Homemade Howitzer

Confirmed by Reliable Eyewitness
Featuring a homemade holiday cannon!

An eyebrow-raising story from an emergency room doctor

5 JULY 2006, OHIO | I was the lucky orthopedics resident on call the night of July 4th. Midnight passed quietly but as dawn broke the next morning, the telephone rang. A fellow was in the trauma unit suffering partial amputation of a finger due to an explosion. I figured that this was a typical firecracker injury and headed over to attend the patient.

I found a gentleman peppered with thousands of black spots—gunpowder embedded in his face, chest, and arms. His left middle finger was essentially missing, and the space between his right thumb and index finger split wide open. His airway was intubated and he also had a chest tube—far more intervention than would be required for a routine firecracker injury.

The man's wife told me what had happened in plain words.

Hubby had built a small cannon in order to celebrate Independence Day. He and his lady both had been drinking heavily throughout the evening. When they regained consciousness the next morning, the gentleman figured he might as well finish off the unused gunpowder. He packed his homemade howitzer, using a cutoff broomstick.

While packing the cannon he was also sucking on a cigarette. Lo and behold, the ash fell and ignited

the powder. The broomstick fired into his chest, ripping through his hands en route as hot gunpowder sprayed out of the cannon.

We took him to the operating room to clean his wounds and complete the amputation. As we removed the stub of his finger, I confided my grave concerns about his future to the attending physician. He looked at me, puzzled. I asked, "How is this man going to be able to drive *without his left middle finger?*"

Reference: Erika Mitchell, MD

Another finger injured in It's The Cure That'll Kill You, *p. 205.*

At-Risk Survivor: Nitrating the Unknown

Confirmed by Reliable Eyewitness
Featuring school, a hammer, and explosions

1970s | Thirty years ago, my college installed new granite tables in the chemistry lab, and somehow a bet got started on who could scratch the tabletop first. The bet went uncollected for a couple of years: Those granite surfaces were pretty sturdy. Then along came my friend, "Mass Destruction."

Armed with an explosive blasting cap and a ball-peen hammer, he was determined to win that bet. Placing the cap on a table, he swung the hammer and hit it squarely. The hammer exited the lab at a high rate of speed over his shoulder. By some fluke, nobody was injured. Mass Destruction did win the bet—the granite was cracked through!

Here is the explanation of how his nickname came about. Earlier that year he had been analyzing an organic sample when the professor came by and casually asked where he was in the procedure.

"I'm nitrating the unknown."

"You didn't get a reaction at the last step?"

"Nope."

It turned out that the professor had added too much denaturing agent to the unknown (glycerin) so it was not identified at the proper stage. Mass Destruction was now casually stirring 250 ml of nitroglycerin on an ice bath! The professor encouraged him to keep stirring—gently—while he evacuated the other students and called the bomb squad.

After the bomb squad had made all the needed arrangements to dispose of the nitroglycerin, they graciously allowed Mass Destruction to push the button on the detonator.

Reference: Anonymous

Darwin wishes to point out that the Nitroglycerine Situation was not the fault of the students, who was working with an "unknown" and trusting teacher.

MICROWAVE SCIENCE

- Take two candy Peeps, arm them with jousting toothpicks and pit them against each other in the microwave.
- Zap a CD on low power to watch the pretty fractal crackle.
- Nuke grape halves to generate balls of plasma.

Home science that is safer than it sounds.

At-Risk Survivor: Against the Odds

Confirmed by Darwin

Featuring an explosive and a vehicle

26 NOVEMBER 2009, DARWIN, AUSTRALIA | Perhaps you wouldn't think twice about bringing a pen or pad of paper home from the office, but an explosive? For six months, a Darwin resident had stored this pilfered "office supply" in his home. Ever since the device had been brought home from work, it had just sat there doing nothing. It seemed so uneventful that the twenty-nine-year-old man admitted to police that he had *driven over it three times* in his motor vehicle, to see what would happen.

Against the odds, nothing!

Bored, he finally contacted Northern Territory police to have the explosive removed from his possession. The officers confirmed that the device was, indeed, a badly crumpled detonator. "It goes without saying," Superintendent J. Emeny contradicted himself, "that any kind of explosive device has the potential to cause serious injury and should be left alone." He added that the man's decision to drive over the device was "risky."

Reference: abc.net.au

At-Risk Survivor: Caps'n'Hammer Kids

Unconfirmed Personal Account
Featuring a hammer, a roll of caps, and a misbehavin' kid

SUMMER 1969 | For the youngsters in the audience, caps are tiny explosive charges sold for use in toy guns. Squeeze the trigger and a striker hits the cap, making it explode with a pop.

I had a pack of caps that were individually "printed" on adhesive-backed paper. Having experimented with using a hammer to detonate them, in true dumb-kid fashion I moved on to supersize it. I stacked the caps an inch and a half high, knelt down on the sidewalk, and hit the stack with a two-pound ball-peen hammer.

The resulting explosion kicked the hammer back clear to my shoulder, missing my fragile young face by inches. No harm except for a bruise on the shoulder and ringing ears, but an alarming near-miss nonetheless.

Sometimes I wonder how any human male survives childhood.

Reference: Anonymous

In a related story . . .

At-Risk Survivor: Pulling the Pin

1967, PENNSYLVANIA | I was nine years old. Fireworks were illegal in our state, but you could buy rolls of caps. A "friend" showed me how to make a decent firecracker out of them. Take a straight pin and load the caps onto it by pushing the point through the center of each powder-loaded circle, folding the paper accordion-style. Fill the pin about half full, then pull the caps off while keeping them as tight together as you can. Wrap the wad in a tissue, twist one end to make a wick, and light the wick for a nice little bang from your homemade firecracker.

Kids all know that bigger is better.

Kids all know that bigger is better. I figured I would use a large pin to make a large firecracker. There was a hatpin in Mom's sewing box and I started loading that colossal pin with a roll of caps. There is no telling how long I worked on that firecracker. I probably had two inches of caps stacked up by the time I was ready to pull them off and wrap the wad in tissue.

I gave the wad a tug, but it wasn't sliding off the pin. I tried harder, still no luck. The head of the pin didn't give me much to hold on to, so I put the pin between my teeth and gave a big tug . . .

That stack of caps exploded with the sound of a shotgun shell. I was standing there with black powder all over my face when my folks and brothers ran into the room. Although my ears were ringing and my lips were tingling, I was required to explain what I had done. Once they stopped laughing, my folks checked to be sure all my parts were still intact.

Fortunately they were!

Reference: Ross Pavlik

At-Risk Survivor: The Mettle of the Kettle

Unconfirmed Personal Account
Featuring explosions and food

The Terrible Teakettle Incident—first time on public view!

Sunday morning I went to the kitchen to make tea, put the kettle on, prepared the cups, and while waiting for the kettle to boil I thought I'd fill my lighter. I got the lighter fuel out, but it was a bit low and quite cold, and it didn't pour well. When this happens, I usually run hot tap water over the can to warm it, but as I already had hot water in the kettle, I decided to steam it for a minute or two.

You can see where this is going, can't you? Wish I had! But I had not yet had my tea, so . . .

I balanced the can on top of the kettle, leaving the kettle lid open. Then I got distracted and the next thing I heard was the sound of the kettle boiling furiously. I turned around just in time to see the fuel container disappear into the mouth of the kettle.

I thought, *Oh dear me!* (or words to that effect) and rushed over to switch off the kettle. I pressed the switch and the gas can let go with a mighty *BANG!* The kettle was instantly transformed into bright yellow, lethal plastic shrapnel.

A few moments after the explosion, I regained my senses sufficiently to realize I was suffering from a deep gash in my thumb, a couple of possibly broken ribs, and one little finger swollen up like a Newmarket sausage. The microwave had a bloody great dent in the side and the kitchen looked like Beirut.

My wife trots to survey the damage, and she says, "If it was the friggin' gas can that did it, where is the friggin' gas can?" At this point I hadn't realized that the can had left the scene of the crime. I looked left—not there. I looked right—not there either. I looked up.

"I think it went thataway!"

There was a neat 50mm hole punched straight through the suspended ceiling. I moved the ceiling panel and found a ragged 75mm hole in the plasterboard above. With the aid of a flashlight, I could see the scorched remains of the can jammed up in the joists, minus top and bottom but otherwise intact.

All the while, I had been bleeding copiously over the remains of the kitchen. I put a Band-Aid on my thumb and had a look at my ribs, which were not broken but sported a kettle-lid-shaped bruise. When I realized that I wasn't seriously damaged and that the house was not in flames, I looked around and saw the funny side and p***ed myself laughing. My wife, however, was not amused.

No sense of humor, some people.

Reference: Barry K.

At-Risk Survivor: Boom Boom Bees

Unconfirmed Personal Account
Featuring explosions, alcohol, and bees!

1999 | Our hero had just moved into a rental home. The yard had not been mowed in more than a year, so he set about mowing down the overgrown weeds and soon ran right over a foot-wide hole. Out came flying a squadron of angry yellowjackets! As he ran in terror, our man knew he had to get rid of these vile pests somehow, and soon.

He sat on the porch pondering the problem over a few brews. As an interim solution, he poured a five-gallon jug of gasoline down the hole, then drank more beer and watched the sun set. What was the likelihood that the mission was accomplished? An hour later he decided to err on the side of caution and burn them out.

He lit a match and tossed it at the hole.

Boom, and I mean *KABOOM!* Hair on arms? Gone! Eyebrows? Gone! Walkway? Cracked, and a six-foot crater where the wasp nest had been. As he stood there, burned and smoking, beer in hand, wife shrieking in the background, he knew . . .

Confession, *I knew* that I had won the Dumbass Award.

Reference: Anonymous

SCIENCE INTERLUDE
EVOLVING CANCER

By Chandra Shekhar

How do we get cancer? In one word, *evolution*.

Toxins, viruses, radiation, errors in DNA copying, and other nasty triggers cause cancerous cells to form in our bodies. Fortunately our immune system kills them off, nipping nascent tumors in the bud. Now and then, however, a few bad cells survive. Multiplying furiously and mutating nonstop, they develop and deploy a vast arsenal of weapons to stay one step ahead of the immune system.

They hide. They sabotage. They subvert. They evade. They attack.

For awhile, the immune system fends them off using its own formidable weaponry. A precarious equilibrium sets in—as fast as the immune system kills the tumor cells, more resistant cells emerge with just the right genetic mix to survive the immune onslaught. At some point, the immune system loses the arms race. Unchecked, the victorious cancer cells run riot, growing in number, invading nearby tissue and spreading to new parts of the body.

The result is a full-blown cancer made of cells that have eluded the immune system time and time again. By allowing only the wiliest tumor cells to survive and grow, the immune system—genetically speaking—*sculpts* the tumor. Such a tumor, in the words of Yale immunologist Richard Flavell, is essentially a Darwinian product.

To defeat cancer, scientists must understand how the immune system tries—and fails—to do so.

Imagine defending a strategic installation—vast, vital, vulnerable—under constant attack by a relentless enemy that grows stronger with every setback. That is precisely the challenge the immune system faces in defending the body from cancer. To have even a hope of success, it must be vigilant, strong, swift, and versatile.

The immune system's first job is to detect the threat. Like a squatter stealing electricity and building materials, a growing tumor remodels the tissue around itself and creates its own blood supply. It does so by exuding chemicals that provoke an inflammation. To the immune system, this chemical Molotov cocktail signals mischief. It sends sentries called natural killer cells to the scene to attack the troublemakers with antitumor compounds. The battle is on.

Cells display bits of protein called *antigens* on their surface. Normal cells display normal antigens that the immune system learns to ignore.

Another type of soldier now enters the fray. The dendritic (den DRIT ik) cell acts as a spy for the immune system. Damaged cells are normally good citizens; they mark themselves for destruction by displaying bits of defective proteins ("antigens") on their surfaces. Dendritic cells gather these antigens from dead tumor cells and go off to alert the rest of the body's defenses.

The alerted immune system then trains a troop of elite commandos—T-cells—for a single mission: Kill all cells sporting these specific tumor antigens. When these new troops arrive at the tumor site, armed and ready, the battle is in full swing.

The immune system is vigilant, strong, and versatile.

Killer T-cells attack tumors using a pair of toxins: one to pierce cells, and the other to kill from within. Besides this one-two punch, T-cells have another strategy: special compounds that send "death signals" to tumor cells, forcing them to commit suicide. Using these weapons, T-cells kill many enemies, replenishing their toxic arsenal as needed. To amplify the attack, these elite commandos multiply at the tumor site, spawning fresh troops. And using trophy antigens taken from their victims, they train the immune system to better attack future cancers of the same type.

Cancer cells don't stand a chance, seemingly.

The reality is quite different. The immune system is indeed vigilant, strong, swift, and versatile. But in cancer, it meets its match. For every immune thrust, cancer has an effective parry, and an equally lethal counterthrust—often turning the immune system's own weapons against it. Here is what it does:

Hide. The immune system expects defective cells to identify themselves using antigens. Not surprisingly, this mechanism is broken in most cancer cells. In some cases, they disguise themselves by displaying only normal cell antigens. In other cases, convenient genetic mutations knock out proteins needed to assemble, transport, or display *any* antigens. Such cancer cells display no antigens at all, neatly flying under the immune radar in stealth mode

Sabotage. Cancers secrete a substance that stops dendritic cells from gathering their antigens, thus hamstringing an effective immune response. They emit a range of other immune-suppressing agents such as vascular endothelial growth factor (VEGF), which not only suppresses the body's defenses, but also helps create a pirate blood supply to feed the growing army of invader cells.

Subvert. Cancers create their own microenvironment that serves as a fortress against attack by the immune system. Using chemical signals, they attract *immature* immune cells from their birthplace in the bone marrow. These callow recruits have not been trained in the immune system's boot camp, and lack antitumor capability—yet their presence repels mature immune cells. Tumors also take hostage a number of regulatory T-cells, suppressing the immune response. Designed to protect normal cells from the immune system, these pacifist regulatory T-cells end up protecting the tumor instead.

Cancer has an effective parry for every immune thrust.

Evade. When asked, well-behaved body cells go peacefully to their graves by triggering an internal self-destruct mechanism. Cancer cells act differently. They often avoid self-destruction by losing cell surface molecules designed to receive death signals from T-cells. Picture a willful child, fingers in ears, saying, *"I don't hear you!"* As a backup, cancer cells manufacture special proteins that break key stages in the self-destruction process. *"You can't make me!"* They also neutralize T-cell toxins with a compound that immune cells themselves use for self-protection.

Attack. Tumors release free radicals, reactive chemicals that weaken or kill immune cells. They secrete compounds that induce natural killer cells to commit suicide or even fratricide. They turn the T-cell's death signal against it, and the T-cell obediently commits suicide—as it tried, and failed, to force the cancer cell to do!

As Professor Flavell puts it, "Cancer has a long, long shopping list of tricks."

Fortunately for us, these tricks are not infallible. Don't tell the tumors, but life may soon get much tougher for them.

Selective evolution notwithstanding, sick cells cannot help but look different from healthy cells. A close scrutiny usually reveals distinctive compounds, or markers, on their surfaces. Once we know the markers for a type of cancer, we can design drugs that precisely attack it. One such drug, *trastuzumab* (Herceptin®), already treats a common type of breast cancer.

Even better, researchers are exploring ways to train the immune system to recognize bad cells by vaccinating with cancer antigens, promoting a stronger, quicker attack. Further, they are designing drugs that help the immune system fight cancer's dirty tricks. These drugs destroy immune-suppressing tumor compounds, recruit immune cells to the tumor, revive weakened immune cells, or force tumor cells to heed death signals.

To the traditional cancer treatments—radiation, surgery, chemotherapy—add another: *immunotherapy*. It is poised to hit the clinic in the near future.

The survival skills of cancer are going to be tested like never before. Can they evolve fast enough to cope with evolving medicine? Stay tuned, and keep your fingers crossed!

REFERENCES:

D. Gabrilovich and V. Pisarev, "Tumor escape from immune response: Mechanisms and targets of activity," *Current Drug Targets* 4(7) (2003), 525–536.

R. Kim, M. Emi, K. Tanabe, "Cancer immunoediting from immune surveillance to immune escape," *Immunology* 121(1) (2007), 1–14.

CHAPTER 4

ELECTRICITY: COMMON GROUNDS

"I know we shouldn't make fun of the misfortunes of others, but I couldn't help myself!"

—Fan mail

Electricity is often the shortest path to a "vivid" demise. Spectacular failures result from the combination of wires, water, and human circuit breakers in a series of spectacular and galvanizing stories. Read onward for amusing and illuminating electrical emergencies.

One Foot in the Pool • An Illuminating Story • Tiny Elec Fence • Electric Bathtub Blues • Tennessee Pee • Shocking Rappel • Shockingly Conductive • Christmas Light Zinger

Darwin Award Winner:
One Foot in the Pool

Confirmed by Darwin
Featuring electricity and water!

24 AUGUST 2008, JAKARTA, INDONESIA | Charles had just completed his International Baccalaureate at King William's College in the Isle of Man. The principal of the college posthumously described him as "a very bright boy with a very bright future." He planned to retire by the age of thirty.

Unfortunately for Charles, his elite education omitted an important lesson from the curriculum: the danger of electricity.

He had one foot in the backyard swimming pool when he noticed a cement box full of electrical wires near the edge of the pool. It was a junction box supplying power to the Jacuzzi. Curious, Charles started to fiddle with a fistful of colored wires and was immediately rooted to the spot by 240 volts of electrical energy surging through his body.

A bright future and early retirement were, indeed, in his cards.

Reference: iomtoday.co.im

Reader Comment

"Charles was a real live wire!"

Darwin Award Winner:
An Illuminating Story

Confirmed by Darwin
Featuring electricity, weather, and a frugal old fart

26 FEBRUARY 2008, FRANCE | A seventy-one-year-old pensioner reached a shocking conclusion when his frugal attempt to illuminate his yard with power siphoned from the National Grid backfired spectacularly.

The gentleman in question illegally opened a major power junction box at the front of his house, intending to hard-wire a cable to his garden shed. Unfortunately he attempted to do this rewiring during a major downpour. The result was all too predictable. The poor chap was immediately rooted to the spot, and declared DART (Darwin Award Right There) at the scene.

Lessons:
1. *Don't* wire your shed to a local power substation.
2. *Don't* wire your shed in the rain.
3. And there is such a thing as being too frugal.

Reference: Ouest-France, rennes.maville.com

Darwin Award Winner: Zap Car*

Confirmed by Darwin

Featuring electricity and vehicles

10 JANUARY 2010, BRAZIL | An electrical discharge made toast of municipal guard Arthur C., forty-seven. According to police reports, he had installed a tiny electric fence around his car to protect against the frequent robberies that occur in his neighborhood in Belém in the state of Pará. Better safe than sorry. Then one evening he forgot that he had left the current on. Let's just say his forgetfulness caused him quite a shock. Galvanic shock.

We are all dying, but some are more eager than others.

Reference: oglobo.globo.com

---

* Zap Car is a play on Zipcar, the laudable car-sharing company with a fleet of low-emisson vehicles.

Historic Darwin Award Winner: Electric Bathtub Blues

Confirmed by Darwin
Featuring electricity, water, and a lightbulb

11 MARCH 1978, FRANCE | The singer Claude François, whose stellar career can be compared to that of legendary Elvis Presley, popularized rock 'n' roll in France. One evening, he returned to his Paris apartment from a busy touring schedule and ran a quiet bath. While standing in the steaming water in the tub, he noticed some wires dangling from the ceiling light. These wires had been the subject of numerous complaints in his various correspondences! The naked singer reached out and grabbed hold of the naked wires . . . and was electrocuted then and there.

Au revoir, Claude.

Reference: Wikipedia and online French TV archives
Researched by the indomitable Ariane La Gauche

Reader Comment

"How do you pronounce that, Claude or Clod?"

Darwin Award Winner: Tennessee Pee

Unconfirmed

Featuring electricity, alcohol, gravity, and bees

1980s, TENNESSEE | A mile down the road from Middle Tennessee State University, a couple of young, very drunk MTSU frat boys climbed a barbed-wire fence that was intended to keep lesser mortals out of an electrical substation. One frat boy climbed right up to the top of a transformer tower. That alone was an obviously bad idea, but it got worse when he urinated on the transformer on which he stood. As if electrocution via genitalia wasn't bad enough, consider his motivating target: a wasp nest attached to the transformer. Needless to say, with electricity and gravity competing for attention, the wasps were the lesser of his worries. He did not live long.

Reference: Anonymous resident of the community

WE CHALLENGE *MYTHBUSTERS*!

Readers skeptical of this story have cited the *MythBusters* episode debunking the so-called myth of peeing on the third rail. However, the large number of incident reports we have received over the years, as well as conversations with reporters and medics, incline us to believe that *people do harm themselves* by urinating on electrified things.

"Coffee Can of Water" from Jim:
"One fact I know: If you scoop up a coffee can of water from a stream next to an electric fence, then pour that water on the fence, you will feel a decent shock through the can. As kids, we dared each other. Now, the next logical dare was, who had the guts to pee on that fence? Nobody ever did, but I am very confident that urine would be as conductive as the water from that stream."

"Herschel the Doberman" from Donna:
"We had been dog-sitting Herschel, an unruly Doberman. When Chris came to pick up Herschel, he hooked the metal chain collar to the metal chain leash and headed outside. Herschel realized it was going to be a long ride home and cocked his leg to take a whiz—right on our electric fence! The electric charge ran up the urine stream, through the metal collar, across the metal leash, and into Chris. Herschel yelped, Chris swore, and both jumped back, breaking the contact. Without question, you can definitely get a charge out of peeing on an electric fence!"

"Sentry Duty" from Jamie:
"During officer training, the pain of digging full-depth trenches in flinty soil was offset by the fun of sentry duty. During the night, the thick fog was regularly punctuated by small blue flashes as returning patrols blundered into the electric fence a farmer had laid along our main fence. Even better was watching people nip out for a pee against a fence post. At some point the spray would hit the live wire, with the same flash and yelp every time!"

At-Risk Survivor: Shocking Rappel

Confirmed by Darwin
Featuring electricity and gravity

1 JUNE 2008, WEST VIRGINIA | In search of altitude, a man climbed the high-voltage power-line tower behind his house, attached a rope to the top of it, and began to rappel down. But he was shocked to discover that his "harmless" hobby was not safe at all when he hit a power line that carries as much as 46,000 volts, according to American Electric Power employees. The man fell to the ground, a battered but lucky survivor of what easily could have been a Darwin-Award-caliber misjudgment.

Reference: *The Charleston Gazette*

Reader Comments

"Thought you'd get a jolt out of this story."
"Now, tell me these stories don't make you feel superior!"

At-Risk Survivor: Shockingly Conductive

Unconfirmed Personal Account
Featuring electricity and a tree!

1971, FLORIDA | An aviation electronics instructor began his class on insulators with this observation: "Wood is a nonconductor, right? Well don't you believe it!"

He had purchased an acre of property that was covered in fast-growing poplar trees, each about five inches thick and twenty feet tall. Ax in hand, he set out to clear the yard. His wife expressed concern about the high-voltage power lines that passed along the edge of the lot, but he assured her that there was nothing to worry about. Wood is nonconductive.

A few minutes later one of his mighty blows felled a tree, which toppled directly onto the power lines. He stood there transfixed as the blue electricity snaked down the tree trunk and up the ax handle, and blew him twenty feet across the yard.

He assured his wife there was nothing to worry about.

Fortunately his wife witnessed the event and rushed his twitching carcass to the hospital, where he was treated for third-degree burns on the palms and soles of his feet (where the electricity entered and exited his body). He was kept in the hospital for two weeks, until his arms quit shaking uncontrollably.

Wood is nonconductive? *Don't you believe it!*

Reference: Carin Gleason

At-Risk Survivor:
Christmas Light Zinger

Unconfirmed Personal Account
Featuring a woman, holiday, and electricity

2009 | I was helping a friend decorate her tree for Christmas. A strand of lights seemed to have a short, so my friend took it upon herself to solve the problem. She stripped the wires in the area and spliced them, and plugged in the lights to check her work. Then she finished up by using her teeth to crimp the bare wires together. Needless to say, she lit up like a Christmas tree!

Reference: Robert Miller

SCIENCE INTERLUDE
QUORUM SENSING: SECRET
LANGUAGE OF BACTERIA

By Adam Mann

The enemy is all around us, invisible, deadly, and using a secret code to coordinate its attacks. In the world of biological warfare, bacteria have humans outnumbered. Not only are there countless combatants on the ground and in the air, but also many species live on and inside our bodies. You are composed of around one trillion human cells, yet at least ten trillion bacteria also call you home. You are more bacteria than human by an order of magnitude!

Although we rarely stop to consider their existence, bacteria are leading intriguing and noisy lives. In recent years, microbiologists have discovered that bacteria possess a useful skill previously thought to be employed only by higher organisms: language.

Scientists call this bacterial language "quorum sensing." Unlike our own speech, it relies solely on simple molecules. With these chemicals, bacteria are able to reach group decisions and coordinate many behaviors, including mass migrations and deadly attacks. Once considered an

WHY DON'T OTHER GROUPS OF BACTERIA, WHEN ONE GROUP GETS TOO STRONG, DO SOMETHING ABOUT THAT GROUP TO PREVENT THAT GROUP FROM DESTROYING THEIR HOST.?!

190   THE DARWIN AWARDS COUNTDOWN TO EXTINCTION

exotic anomaly, quorum sensing recently has been discovered in nearly all bacteria. Every species has its own vocabulary to prevent eavesdropping by neighboring bacteria, though their languages are as closely related as Spanish is to Italian.

Quorum sensing works like this: An individual bacterium constantly releases a particular chemical into its environment, telling its brethren, "I'm here!" Other bacteria of the same species hear this message while releasing their own "I'm here!" chemical. The bacteria sense the concentration of that chemical and are thus able to estimate how many of their siblings are in the immediate surroundings. Armed with this information, they make decisions based on their quantity.

For humans, bacterial quorum sensing can be deadly.

For example, a lone member of a life-threatening species might get into your body. By itself, it stands no chance of evading your immune system and taking you down. Producing toxins, or doing anything except laying low in such an environment, would be a waste of energy.

But there is strength in numbers. Over time, the bacterium multiplies, and perhaps a few more sneak into your body, each loudly announcing its presence while multiplying furiously. Soon enough, there is a whole bacterial chorus shouting to the world of their arrival. Once the bacteria have massed enough troops to take you down, they begin their attack and pump out toxins. You get sick. Without treatment, you may die.

While the scenario seems dire, understanding quorum sensing is giving researchers hope. Biologists are learning how to decode this bacterial language and produce chemical tools that "jam" some of the communication lines. *This method is a brand-new tactic in the fight against antibiotic resistance.* Quorum sensing evolved billions of years ago, so it is likely to be much harder for bacteria to develop immunity to these weapons, compared to the relative ease of defeating traditional antibiotics.

> Scientists are now manufacturing molecules that silence the bacterial dialogue, turning the bacteria's advantage into a disadvantage.

Antibiotic-resistant bacteria are a serious problem worldwide. Our reliance on penicillin, ampicillin, and other antibiotics—while lifesaving—has produced some nasty strains of killers. For instance, one of the most well-studied quorum-sensing bacteria is the opportunistic *Pseudomonas aeruginosa*. Some strains are highly resistant to antibiotics, and this microbe is often responsible for nosocomial infections—pneumonia and wound infections acquired during a patient's stay in a hospital.

P. aeruginosa colonies are clever. They signal to one another when a host's white blood cells are on the march and, as a group, produce a chemical that eliminates the white blood cells, disabling a patient's immune system. And once these shrewd bugs know that they've reached high density in a body they can enter into a state known as a biofilm, a gooey layer of germs and proteins that acts as a shield against antibiotics.

But, by knowing which chemicals are used to coordinate this conspiracy, doctors may someday gain the upper hand and turn the *P. aeruginosa* deaf to their comrades. Without speech, individual bacteria will no longer be able to go about their trickery. This could be a huge boon to hospital patients, particularly immune-compromised ones such as those with AIDS or undergoing radiation therapy.

Aside from medical applications, there are many interesting complexities to quorum sensing.

A microbe never lives alone: A diverse jungle of species usually surrounds it. While each has its own language, there is a second system—a bacterial *lingua franca*—that allows all species to communicate with one another. Referred to as quorum-sensing cross talk, this scheme allows bacteria to measure the total amount of other species in their neighborhood. Researchers are just beginning to understand this cross talk, which could allow species to make decisions together based on the local environment.

Furthermore, using genetic analysis, researchers discovered that bacteria have been "speaking" for far longer than we have. Quorum sensing is so widespread in bacteria that it must have evolved billions of years ago and provided such a survival advantage that it stuck around. By studying the genetic changes that control quorum sensing, scientists will be able to trace lineages and better understand bacterial evolution.

In fact, since quorum sensing has been around for so long, it means that we multicellular creatures came into being against a chattering background. Some scientists believe that learning about bacterial communication will give insight into how our own cells organize into tissues and organs, a process that obviously involves close coordination.

As humans, we sometimes think of ourselves as standing on the top rung of the evolutionary ladder. But all organisms have an equally long history. Humans aren't so exalted, evolutionarily speaking, and lowly bacteria routinely humble us with their highly attuned chemical signaling.

Bacteria were here first, and they set the rules. Perhaps if we

AND WITH THEIR STUPIDITY! ALLOWING ONE BAD APPLE STRAIN TO KILL OFF THE HOST AND SUDDENLY THEM ALL!

learn to speak their language, we will alter the rules enough to help ourselves. But we should never forget that the ones in charge are the smallest. The meek shall inherit the earth; in fact, they already have.

For more information, visit the University of Nottingham's quorum-sensing site:

http://nottingham.ac.uk/quorum

CHAPTER 3

TOOLS: THE MONKEY WRENCH

"When you tempt fate . . ." Man is called the tool-using animal. So what do we call a man who misuses tools? Well, much of the time we call him a Darwin Award Winner. The human animal is remarkably creative in finding ways to mishandle everything from a basic shovel to more sophisticated tools like chainsaws, drills, air compressors, washing machines, and Tasers. Wait! Don't touch that knob . . .

*Fool's Gold • Rub the Mint • Saw It Coming! • A Drilliant Idea •
It's the Cure That'll Kill You • Spin Cycle • A Putty Bullet*

Darwin Award Winner: Fool's Gold

Confirmed by Darwin
Featuring money and a shovel

5 FEBRUARY 2009, INDIA | Bachelor lottery agent Pravin K. lived with his brother's family in Vasai. His own house, an abandoned hundred-year-old building, was located a few meters away.

Some legends hold that a pot of gold lies buried at the end of the rainbow, but Pravin learned in a dream that an ancient pot of gold was actually buried beneath his house! He decided to "follow his dreams" and dig for that gold. He kept his plans private to avoid a fight over the fortune.

The dream told him to dig beneath the staircase, so after lunch every day without fail, Pravin would take his spade and dig a little deeper beneath the stairs. The neighbors had no idea that days and nights of digging had resulted in a long, fifteen-foot-deep tunnel. The innovative gold digger had even rigged a remote-control toy car to carry a flashlight to assist him in the dark!

He was smart enough to control his lighting needs, but not smart enough to take into account the water table. One day the thirty-two-year-old lottery agent did not return home, and his worried relatives lodged a missing persons report. Police discovered that the floor of the old house had caved in. The soil beneath the staircase becomes wet at a depth of five meters due to its proximity to the sea, and the unsupported walls of the tunnel had collapsed.

A few hours later an earthmover excavated Pravin's body from the debris, along with a spade and the innovative mobile flashlight. The lottery agent's number . . . was up.

Reference: *Mumbai Mirror*

BEACH GETAWAY

Digging a hole sounds simple enough but it's actually a dangerous activity.

Sunny, sandy beaches can get crowded, even on a winter day. In December 1997, a quest for privacy and protection from the wind prompted D. Jones to dig an eight-foot-deep hole on the beach in Buxton, North Carolina. He unfolded a beach chair at the bottom of the pit, and was enjoying his hard-won seclusion when the wet sand collapsed, burying him in a suffocating slide. Although digging for privacy—or for gold—may seem to be a harmless pastime, distinct danger lurks in the depths of a deeply dug hole.

Reference: *Darwin Awards 4: Intelligent Design*
(Plume, 2007)

Darwin Award Winner: Rub the Mint

Unconfirmed Personal Account
Featuring school, work, and an air compressor!

DECEMBER 1988, ROMANIA | I was a student of electricity and mechanics in Communist Romania. At the time, it was mandatory for all children, including university students, to boost the economy by "active participation." Each autumn we worked in agriculture, harvesting fruits and vegetables, and for three weeks per year we were required to train in a power plant or factory, to get a feel for successful Communist industry. This was known as "Rub the Mint."

My class was sent to Slatina where aluminum was obtained with the power-hungry electrolysis process. We were not much use, so we were ignored by the people in charge of our training. We spent our copious down time reviewing our class notes. Not only were the students bored, but so were many workers in the factory, who were actually paid for doing nothing.

One day I was assigned to walk documents from one department to another. Along the way, I spotted two men crafting a wooden coffin. I was accustomed to all kinds of crazy sights, but a coffin . . . ? Was the aluminum factory branching out into funeral supplies?

"The coffin is for a comrade who accidentally removed himself from the gene pool," the woodcrafters told me. And how had this accident come to pass?

Two men in their twenties, recent hires, were fiddling with the pressurized air hose used to power

He did not believe his comrade would be so stupid as to proceed.

industrial air tools. They swept the dust off their dusty clothes, and this was so much fun that one of them dropped his pants to feel the air sweep across his testicles. He bent over further, and bet his comrade that he had the guts to pressurize his guts, and maybe experience some fun farts.

He proceeded to stick the hose in his anus and release six bar (atmospheres) of pressure, inflating and rupturing his intestines.

He died within minutes from internal hemorrhage. Even if he had been goofing off in a hospital corridor, he would not have survived: Several meters of his colon and intestines had ruptured.

The employee was posthumously found to have broken internal (heh) company regulations. His "scientific collaborator" stated that he did not believe his comrade would be so stupid as to proceed and thought he was only goofing off.

Reference: Florin Ungureanu, who says it wasn't covered in the media because it happened during Communist times

Fun fact: In powdered form, aluminum catches fire quickly when exposed to a flame.

INDUSTRIAL SCIENCE

Aluminum is a very important metal in modern society. The main natural source of aluminum is aluminum oxide, Al_2O_3, a very stable compound. You can't extract the aluminum just by heating the oxide—you need more energy.

The Electrolytic Process

A method of smelting aluminium was discovered in 1886 by Charles Martin Hall, a twenty-one-year-old college student. The aluminum oxide is melted, and forms ions of aluminum and oxygen. A positive and a negative electrode are immersed in the molten liquid, and electrical current (a flow of electrons) flows out of the cathode. Positively charged aluminum ions pick up negatively charged electrons and deposit on the cathode as pure aluminum metal, while oxygen gas combines with the anode to form carbon dioxide gas.

The melting point of aluminum oxide is more than 2,000°C. Modern smelters save energy by dissolving a small amount of aluminum oxide in cryolite (Na_3AlF_6) which melts at a much lower temperature, closer to 1,000°C. An electrical current is passed through this molten mixture and, as described above, aluminum ions combine with electrons to form liquid aluminum metal that is siphoned from the bottom of the tank. The oxygen ions combine with carbon from the anode to form carbon dioxide, CO_2 (which is much safer than O_2).

Merits Discussion: Saw It Coming!

Confirmed—Or Is It?

Featuring electricity, alcohol, and a chainsaw!

27 JUNE 2009, NEW YORK | A severe storm damaged power lines and left seventeen thousand homes without electricity. Mieczysław M., sixty-four, was one of the affected parties. His power line serviced only seventeen homes and therefore was one of the last to be repaired. Seven hours after the line fell, the disgruntled man finally lost his patience.

The old man had been shooed away repeatedly by firefighters who were guarding the power line. "Police and firefighters literally chased him away, did everything [they] could," said the Sullivan County commissioner of public safety. But they were not prepared for the homeowner's sudden bold move.

Mieczysław emerged from his home shortly after midnight with an industrial power saw in his hands and plastic bags on his feet. He stood in a puddle of water and attempted to saw through a 4,800-volt feeder line that was dangling off the pole. One thing led to another, and soon he was on intimate terms with the hissing and buzzing live wire. While emergency responders waited for utility workers to shut down the power, Mieczysław was busy dancing his way to death's door.

The story says it all. The old coot was repeatedly shooed away from the power line but insisted on cutting it while standing in a puddle, and now he is safely out of the gene pool. Thanks for doing our species a favor, Mieczysław!

Reference: Middletown *Times Herald-Record*, YWN Sullivan County News Team,
Mid-Hudson News Network, and an anonymous NYSEG employee

MERITS DEBATED!

News reports spelled his name Mieczyskaw, but that name is
not listed in the Social Security Death Database. There is an
obituary for Mieczyslaw M. (note spelling difference) at
findagrave.com, stating that he died—not in 2009—but in
2008. Ultimately we concluded that the man did indeed exist,
at least before his feud with the power line. This common Polish
surname is difficult to spell correctly, and the discrepancy at
findagrave.com is likely due to the fact that contributors submit
unverified new listings.

Still, things are not adding up. Industrial saws require power,
but the power was out! Was it a gas-powered or cordless circular
saw? Besides, a fallen line doesn't just sit there hissing for seven
hours; a fuse blows or is pulled at the site by the utility company.
And why would anyone take a saw to a downed electric line?
This certainly will not restore power. If the old guy was mental,
he would be disqualified based on Rule #4: Maturity.

A polish reader suspects he was displaying a national trait: a
perverted sense of justice. "Fair" is when everyone is doing
equally badly, so perhaps he saw fit to deprive the *whole area*
of electricity since his house still lacked it.

The merits of this nomination are still being debated:
www.DarwinAwards.com/book/seesaw

At-Risk Survivor: A Drilliant Idea

Confirmed by Darwin
Featuring spray paint, fire, and a drill

13 JUNE 2009, WASHINGTON | A Spokane man with a spray paint can learned the wrong way to get around a clogged nozzle. Fire officials say the man used a cordless drill to penetrate the pressurized can. The contents spewed out of the hole, and a small spark from the drill ignited a flash fire. The man's face was seriously burned, but he was treated at the Deaconess Medical Center and lived to spray another day.

Reference: *The Spokesman-Review*

TAG! YOU'RE IT.

In 2002 another paint-bespattered person met Mr. Darwin. An electric train roof was suffering from a bad case of the flames. After fire crews extinguished the blaze, they found a puzzling lump of charcoal. Was it involved in the fire? The answer: Yes, and rather intimately. Hours before the blaze, this lump had walked right past high voltage warning signs, surmounted fences, and climbed onto the roof of a train to spray-paint his graffiti masterpiece. When he finished, he stood and raised his arms in triumph—and touched the 15,000-volt main power line. The electrical current permanently revoked his artistic license and incinerated the flammable wet paint of his final masterpiece.

At-Risk Survivor:
It's the Cure That'll Kill You

Confirmed by Reliable Eyewitness
Featuring women, a snake, and a Taser

11 MAY 2008, CALIFORNIA | Working in a hospital's emergency room can be described as periods of frenetic activity punctuated by moments of boredom. During the latter, I was explaining the nuances necessary for a truly good Darwin Award, and the extraordinary effort it takes to win one. As an example I referenced a truly bizarre occurrence in our own little hospital. Three of us were on duty on Mother's Day in the ER when a pitiful woman was brought in suffering from a venomous snakebite to her right hand.

> **She spotted a small brown snake . . .**

The fifty-three-year-old had been strolling with her family in celebration of the holiday, when she spotted a small brown snake that she misidentified as a garter snake. To her credit, everyone involved agreed that the snake had no rattles, but the fact that it SHOULD HAVE is indisputable. She was bitten on the middle finger, and the immediate pain and swelling alerted the group to the fact of a serious envenomation. This is all too common a story, but what ensued raises its novelty value.

Our little city of Ojai has a well-deserved reputation as a hotbed of alternative healing, unique lifestyles, and New Age philosophy. Still, the ER staff were surprised to hear the family's account of their treatment for their mother. Someone in the group had heard a rumor that Tasers would counter the effect of a rattlesnake bite. Unfortunately this family *did* have access to a Taser weapon, and they zapped their poor mother!

When the pain and swelling continued advancing up her arm, they did the only sensible thing: They Tasered Mom again. With little else in their armamentarium, or perhaps running low on batteries, they brought Mom to the emergency room—where they expressed considerable dismay as the staff ignored the Taser idea and proceeded to treat her with antivenom (standard snakebite care) and admit her to the ICU.

Antivenom is purified from serum taken from an animal that has been injected with tiny amounts of venom to provoke an immune response. The antibodies bind to and neutralize the toxin molecules, halting further damage. Antivenom must be administered ASAP because it does not reverse damage already done. Historically, immunized horses were the animal of choice, but today sheep and goats are more common sources of antivenom because there is less chance of serum sickness caused by an immune response to the animal's antigens.

All ended well, even for the snake, rendering this just an anecdote among the truly terminal stories collated by Darwin. And for those still in doubt about the efficacy of a Taser against snake venom . . . thanks for the job security!

Reference: Anonymous MD;
Ojai Hospital Medical Records

At-Risk Survivor: Spin Cycle

Unconfirmed Personal Account
Featuring holiday fun, fireworks, and a washing machine!

4 JULY 2008 | Two coworkers decided to celebrate the 4th of July in their own special way. They loaded an old washing machine with tens of pounds of firecrackers, lit a fuse, dropped the lid, and ran . . . Nothing happened. Twenty minutes later, they decided that the fuse was a dud and went back to try again.

Presumably neither was aware of the chemical friendship between oxygen and fire. As they lifted the lid the entire washer-load of fireworks exploded, landing them both in the hospital for several days. Shrapnel from the washer spread in a twenty-five-foot radius, leaving a large crater in its wake. Considering the size of the impact crater, each perpetrator suffered relatively minor wounds and burns.

They decided that the fuse was a dud.

Reference: Lisa Perry

In 1998, two East Java villagers took a creative approach to celebrating the feast that marks the end of Ramadan. They purchased a large quantity of firecrackers on the black market, twisted the fuses into a rope, and connected the rope to a motorcycle battery. When they started the engine, the resulting explosion could be heard two kilometers away!

At-Risk Survivor:
A Putty Bullet

Confirmed by Darwin

Featuring a gun

12 MARCH 2009, OKLAHOMA | A Shawnee-area marksman suffered an accidental gunshot wound when he fired a round of Plumber's Putty into his own abdomen. The twenty-one-year-old explained to deputies that he had exchanged the BB pellets in shotgun shells for putty and test fired several rounds outside. Satisfied, he decided to perform more tests on the modified projectiles.

For instance, what would happen if he put a pillow between himself and the gun? He allegedly shot himself with no problem. Then he tried the experiment *without* the pillow. He was taken to Unity Health Center for injuries to his abdomen, shirt, and winter coat. Removal of the wad (a plastic shell component that encloses the pellets) may eventually be necessary, but otherwise he survived the navel piercing no worse for the wear.

The young man admitted that "something went wrong."

But what? Sheriff's Captain Palmer pointed out the obvious. "Shotgun shells and Plumber's Putty don't mix."

Reference: Pottawatomie County Sheriff Archive; *The Shawnee News-Star*

Reader Comments

"Silly Putty."

"Putty-Putty Bang Bang"

"Guns don't shoot people, people shoot people."

"A shotgun is rather long. Did he pull the trigger with his toes? Was it a sawed-off shotgun?"

"Perhaps the soft 'rubber' bullets were intended to drive away trespassers without causing injury—so through a series of somewhat scientific experiments he tested the device on himself."

"At Harvey Mudd College in 1990, North Dorm's motto—Piss on East—was taken verbatim by the occasional group of North-dormers. Someone in East Dorm decided to string a defensive electric wire across the outer perimeter. Of course, *he tested it first* to make sure it was safe . . ."

SCIENCE INTERLUDE
RAPID EVOLUTION

By Jane Palmer

If the human race is suffering from terminal information overload, there is worse to come: We're going to have to do more with less. Our brains are shrinking.

It's true. Or at least our skulls are shrinking. Take the mammoth skull of Robert the Bruce, the fourteenth-century king who freed Scotland from the grip of the English. Nearly twenty centimeters long, sixteen centimeters wide across the forehead, Bruce's sturdy skull was designed to take a bash or two—which it most likely got from the vengeful English.

Robert the Bruce is not alone in his massive brain box.* Our predecessors have us beaten when it comes to skull size. Five thousand years ago our skulls were approximately 150 cubic centimeters larger than they are now—the size of a large bag of M&M's—able to house 10 percent more brains!

————

* Who else is in there?

Heads Are Not All That Are A-Changing

A dwindling brain is just one of a plethora of changes taking place in our species in recent history. Humans are evolving faster than ever before, picking up new traits and talents to deal with an equally fast-changing environment. This gives birth to the concept of rapid evolution—*rapid* and *evolution* being two words you never expected to see in the same sentence.

Human evolution, anthropologists say, accelerated a hundredfold in the past ten thousand years. Ironically even evolution has to keep up with the pace of life.

Shrinking brains were a big surprise. But a hundred-fold increase in the speed of evolution is almost inconceivable! To come to this startling conclusion, anthropologists themselves had to evolve from a group obsessed with skeletons, to one that also fully embraces molecular technology. Today the skeleton geeks are sifting through not only dirt, but also DNA sequences to find point mutations (affecting a single nucleotide) that show just when various evolutionary changes took place.

Lobe finned fish, the famous fish that first crawled onto land, lived in ponds subject to seasonal drought. Fleshy fins allowed them to "walk" from drying pools to deeper water, and the swim bladder evolved into a sac able to breathe air. Lobe finned fish are the ancestors of amphibians and all higher types of vertebrates, including man.

How can scientists tell how old a particular mutation is? One hundred years old—or older than before our genome diverged from the ape or the lobe-finned-fish? Luckily there's a giveaway.

The Molecular Clock

Each mutation has "hitchhiking neighbors" nearby—in science jargon, juxtaposed genes—that, like our own neighbors, simply happen to live close to one another. When our diploid chromosomes recombine into haploid eggs or sperm, any given piece of DNA usually sorts out with its nearby neighbors. In each generation, the probability of two neighbors being shuffled apart is low. Only over time do the neighboring DNA sequences separate.

Scientists observe how many hitchhiking neighbors are associated with a mutation, and compare results from different samples. If many common neighbors are founds, the mutation is recent. If not, then the mutation is older and its neighborhood has changed over a period of time. This is the so-called **molecular clock.** We share *most* of our juxtaposed genes with other humans, *many* of our juxtaposed genes with apes, and *some* of our juxtaposed genes with the lobe-

> **Molecular Clock:** the DNA surrounding a point mutation that reveals whether the mutation is recent, ancient, or somewhere in between

finned fish that lived 400 million years ago, By cross-referencing this information with data obtained from the fossil record, we can date when each mutation, point by point, changed us from fish to amphibian, monkey to man.

Now let's turn the molecular clock forward, and shed some light on the modern day. When this phenomenally informative tool was applied to a large collection of human

DNA, the HapMap Database*, we discovered that hundreds of genes have changed in the last ten thousand years. In fact, small or large changes occurred in approximately 7 percent of all human genes. That's a lot!

If evolution had been ticking steadily at the current rate for the last six million years—since humans and chimpanzees separated—there would be 160 times more differences between us and the chimps than we actually observe. Pretty weird, huh? Evolution used to be slower, and it's speeding up!

What is driving this whirlwind of genetic activity?

It turns out that behind the accelerated rate of evolution are two familiar forces: civilization and a population explosion.

Nobody farmed, milked animals, or lived in cities thirteen thousand years ago. Vast changes in cultures and ecological niches have resulted in new opportunities for adaptation. Our genes had to hustle to enable us to survive and thrive in all that chaos called "civilization."

Add to that an unrelenting drive to reproduce that has increased our population from millions to billions in the last ten thousand years. More people means more mutation opportunities.

---

* HapMap Project: A catalog of genetic differences among populations around the world. Three million point mutations have been identified; medical advances are one of the many benefits expected to emerge from the HapMap Project. ScienceDaily has a fascinating article about the project: http://tinyurl.com/23qpymp

Malaria, Milk, and Earwax

Peek inside the human body and check out some recent mutations. Some we can explain, others are still mysteries.

In Africa, India, and Pakistan, where inhabitants face the long-standing and pervasive threat of malaria, 10–15 percent of the population has evolved resistance to the disease. This resistance developed within the last four thousand years, in the unlikely form of the gene for sickle cell anemia. The same gene that damages red blood cells, resulting in life-threatening tissue damage, also prevents the malaria parasite from turning innocent blood cells into malaria factories. Our new genetic defense is a double-edged sword.

Eight thousand years ago, the gene that enabled adults to digest milk first made its appearance in Europe. This mutation is a simple regulatory change that allows lifelong production of the infant enzyme lactase. The ability to digest milk from cradle to grave suddenly made dairy a rich source of food for adults. Dairy farming became such a wildly successful means of feeding your family that the "dairy gene" quickly spread. How quick is quick? After eight thousand years, approximately 95 percent of the German population has the gene, as well as the Masai in Africa and the Lapps in Finland.

Earwax is on the wane.

Endemic malaria and the advent of dairy farming have associated mutations that show how environments mold our genes, but the rationale for some mutations is still baffling. Hop over to Asia where we find rapidly spreading genes that suppress body odor and earwax! Less sweat could conceivably offer a slight benefit in cold climates, but no scientist yet has claimed to understand what survival advantage *less earwax* might confer.

Our scientists are searching for human mutations big and small, from those involving the onset of speech to those that might impact Q-tip sales. From a genetic vantage point, we are finding that the human race resembles a diverse cluster of weird mutants. But one new evolutionary trend is shared between populations in Asia, Europe, Africa, Australia, Anerica, and every country where anthropologists have been able to take calipers: The human skull is shrinking, even as our bodies grow.

WENDY'S SEXY NEIGHBOR NOTION

If an advantageous mutation occurs, the neighborhood around that mutation is selected for too. So something really great like **X-Ray vision** or the ability to **smell flowers** can be linked to something meaningless, like green eyes. *We can track some beneficial mutations just by looking at associated visible traits.* Imagine that green eyes were linked to a wildly successful mutation allowing the immune system to defeat cancer*. How many generations would it take before we notice that the healthiest people are green-eyed? How long before they are sought as wives and husbands for their longer life spans? If eye color becomes a *marker* for improved health, how long before the marker itself is considered sexy?

---

* See "Evolving Cancer" (p. 171) for more about the battles our bodies wage against cancer.

Whether our intelligence is also shrinking is a question for debate. When it comes to our cerebral cortex, size isn't everything—Albert Einstein and Anatole France, the infamous French novelist, were both pea-brained geniuses. But even if our wits are waning, in a world where you can outsource many of your mental tasks to a computer, and where the onslaught of modern media rewards those with the attention span of a gnat, the downsizing of our intellect could be a huge plus. Big brains are expensive to make and maintain, and if Mother Nature can get by with less—she will.

We could be evolving rapidly toward idiocracy.

REFERENCES:

I. J. Deary et al., "Skull size and intelligence, and King Robert Bruce's IQ," *Intelligence* 35 (2007), 519–525.

J. Hawks et al., "Recent acceleration of human adaptive evolution." *Proc Nat Acad Sci* 104 (December 2007) http://tinyurl.com/rapid-evolution.

John Hawks, "Rapid evolution: Can mutations explain historical events?" *New Horizons in Science* (2009).

Arthur Keith, "The brain of Anatole France," *The British Medical Journal* 2 (349) (1927), 1048–1049.

CHAPTER 2
RANDOM ACTS OF RIDICULOUSNESS

"Remember, they do it to themselves . . ."

Introducing a smorgasbord of creative demises: Slide down a mountainside, zip across a glacier, paint your face, ride the storm, be a ninja, hide in a locker, get "up close and personal" with a tennis machine! Darwin himself never could have dreamed up such inventive ways of skimming debris from the gene pool.

Sparkleberry Lane • Sky Surfers • Sky Rider • A Shoe-In Winner • Race to the Bottooommm • Glacier Erasure • Locker Room Humor • Ninja Wannabe • Birch Slapped • Tennis Blow • An Un-Fun Whirlwind • Medieval Mayhem

Darwin Award Winner: Sparkleberry Lane

Confirmed by Darwin

Featuring criminals and spray paint!

This could be a breakthrough in crime prevention . . .

31 JULY 2009, SOUTH CAROLINA | Two disguised men entered a Sprint store on Sparkleberry Lane, pulled out guns, and stole wallets, purses, and credit cards from employees before ordering them into a bathroom. Both men fled, but they could not flee from their own stupidity. Twenty-three-year-old James T. had disguised himself by painting his face gold.

Yes, in order to conceal his identity during the robbery, James had covered his skin with metallic spray paint. If this isn't a Darwin Award, what is? Paints are clearly labeled: DO NOT GET ON SKIN, DO NOT GET IN EYES, DO NOT INHALE. Paint fumes are well-known to be toxic, and the metallic colors are particularly noxious. James began having trouble breathing (surprise!) and died wheezing shortly after the robbery took place.

To add insult to injury, the disguise was ineffective. Witnesses were certain as to the identity of their assailant. Had he lived, James, like his surviving accomplice, would have been charged with armed robbery.

Reference: wistv.com, *The* (South Carolina) *State*

Darwin Award Winner: Sky Surfer

Confirmed by Darwin
Featuring kites, weather, and machismo!

OCTOBER 2007, IBIZA, SPAIN | Storm winds swept across southern Spain, causing widespread flooding and damage to buildings along the Costa Blanca. *Tasty waves*, thought one intrepid kite surfer as he packed his gear and hit the beach.

Move over, Charlie Brown. Today's large kites are not triangles held by a string, helpless fodder for kite-eating trees. Modern kites are controlled by multiple lines with surface areas that create so much lift that it can be difficult to keep your feet planted on the ground—even during normal wind conditions. These were not normal conditions. Heavy rainstorms, flooding, and landslides had caused the government to declare a state of emergency and close the beaches.

Good times, thought the forty-year-old Spanish surfer as he unfurled his kite, climbed onto his board, and embarked on the ride of a lifetime. The high winds picked him up and ultimately carried him almost a kilometer inland, tagging him against buildings along the way.

One more nominee joins the queue to meet Charles Darwin . . . in person.

Reference: Spain RTVE, neurope.eu, *Deutsche Presse-Agentur*

At-Risk Survivor: Sky Rider

Confirmed by Darwin

18 AUGUST 2008, FLORIDA | A news crew was filming a storm when they captured footage of a twenty-six-year-old man kite boarding on the winds of Tropical Storm Fay. Harnessed to his sail, he was picked up by the wind and playfully slammed into the beach. His harness was equipped with emergency releases, but the wind whirled him around so fast that he had no time to jettison the kite. The wind continued its pranks, dragging him along the sand, picking him up again, and bashing him into a building.

A witness said, "It was a miracle that he just flew over the street and didn't get hit by a car" during his aerial adventure. The man's family described him an experienced kite boarder; one might even consider him over-experienced! The happy-go-lucky surfer survived to play another day.

This story calls to mind the Doors' song "Riders on the Storm."

Reference: cbs4.com

Darwin Award Winner:
A Shoe-In

Confirmed by Darwin

Featuring trains and machismo

15 DECEMBER 2009, GERMANY | A U2 subway driver found a body laying besides the underground tracks in Berlin. Because there was no video surveillance camera at that location, it took police two days to reconstruct what had happened. Apparently Yasin A., twenty-two, was alone in the subway car when he decided it would be a brilliant idea to destroy one of the windows. By swinging feet forward from a handrail into the window, he not only managed to burst the glass but also succeeded in being sucked out of the moving train, and was left dead on the tracks.

He was alone in the compartment at the time; if an observer had been present, perhaps the young underground rider would not have engaged in the destructive nonsense that led to his senseless death.

Reference: BZ Berlin

Darwin Award Winner: Race to the Bottooommm

Confirmed by Darwin
Featuring machismo versus gravity!

5 SEPTEMBER 2009, OREGON | Jake reached the summit of Saddle Mountain, and there and then he informed his friends that he planned to make a controlled slide down the cliff face. He would meet up with them in the parking lot or on the trail below.

Some folks are satisfied with the risks and rewards of dune sliding, and the chance of a 150-foot broken-limb tumble. Not Jake. The eighteen-year-old decided to "git-r-dun" down a thousand-foot cliff, instead. He slid pell-mell down the escarpment—and what was intended to be a controlled rockslide ended abruptly a thousand feet below the summit, when his body came to rest in a steep ravine.

Friends were shocked. "We are shocked," they said, "because he is *always doing stuff like this* and coming out smiling."

Reference: OregonLIVE.com

Reader Comments

"What a downer."

"Why daredevils don't live long."

"Rocky Mountain Low."

Darwin Award Winner:
Glacier Erasure

Confirmed by Reliable Eyewitness
Featuring weather, hunting, and gravity!

In the late fall and early winter months, snow-covered mountains become infested with hunters. One ambitious pair climbed high up a mountain in search of their quarry. The trail crossed a small glacier that had crusted over, and the lead hunter had to stomp a foothold in the snow one step at a time, in order to cross the glacier.

Somewhere near the middle of the glacier, his next stomp hit not snow but a rock. The lead hunter lost his footing and fell. Down the crusty ice he zipped, off the edge and out of sight. Unable to help, his shocked companion shouted out, "Are you OK?"

"Yes!" came the answer.

Reasoning that it was a quick way off the glacier, the second hunter plopped down and accelerated down the ice, following his friend. There, just over the edge, was his friend . . . holding on to the top of a tree that barely protruded from the snow.

There were no other treetops nearby, nothing to grab, nothing but a hundred-foot drop onto the rocks below. As the second hunter shot past the first, he uttered his final epitaph: a single pithy word.

Reference: The archives of an MD with thirty years of experience in the ER

Reader Comments

"Truly a slippery slope."

"O'er the glacier and through the snow . . . Whoa! *Look out below.*"

"I think the world would be . . . biological."

"Now this would be a winter Olympics sport I would watch!"

At-Risk Survivor:
Locker Room Humor

Confirmed

Featuring alcohol and claustrophobia

17 JULY 2009, GERMANY | Unexpected odds 'n' ends are always turning up in train station lockers, but this may be the oddest yet. After a night spent carousing with friends, squeezing into the Ludwigshafen train station locker had seemed like an amusing idea to the man. He shut himself in a suitcase locker for fun, but the laughter faded as the oxygen supply dwindled. His companions were unable to open the locked door and free the twenty-year-old! With time running out, police broke open the door and dragged the groggy prankster to safety.

Our alert readers ask, "Just *why* did they let him out . . . ?"

Reference: Reuters

At-Risk Survivor: Ninja Wannabe

Confirmed by Darwin
Featuring machismo

Michelangelo would never meet this fate.

16 NOVEMBER 2009, WASHINGTON | Seattle police were searching for a reported assault victim when they heard screams of pain and followed their ears to a grisly scene: a man impaled on a fence post! They supported him to prevent further injuries until fire department personnel arrived to stabilize him and transport him to a hospital.

Suspecting that he was the victim in the reported assault, officers interviewed Vlad the Impaled (his name was not released) in his hospital bed. The man insisted that he was *not* being chased, but rather thought he was a ninja and could successfully vault a five-foot spiked fence. The man's mad ninja skills, it seems, were bested by the fence—and he ended up stuck like a pig.

"Clearly he was overconfident in his abilities."

He is no Darwin Award winner, merely an At-Risk Survivor. His skewered carcass was in serious but stable condition in intensive care when last we checked. A police spokesman summarized the situation: "Clearly he was overconfident in his abilities."

Reference: *Seattle Post-Intelligencer,* AP, msnbc.com

At-Risk Survivor: Birch Slapped

Unconfirmed Personal Account
Featuring trees and gravity

11 JULY 2009, NEW YORK | On a ten-day camping trip deep in the Adirondacks, a guide noticed a dead birch leaning toward one of the tents. This was dangerous! The guide enlisted three members of the church group to help deal with the tree situation.

Somehow our hero missed the memo. First they tried pushing the fifty-foot tree over—it was leaning at quite an angle—but that had no effect whatsoever. Then they whacked at it with trekking poles, but that only scraped up the bark. Finally they decided that the only alternative was to pull down the tree.

The guide removed the haul line from the bear bag and threw it over a short branch halfway up the tree. By pulling on each end of the line, they planned to wedge the dead tree against a sturdy live tree that was situated well away from the tent. They figured that this would avoid damage to the campsite.

Now the plan was to put two people on each end of the rope, pull as hard as possible until they heard the wood crack, then let go and run away from the falling tree. But somehow our hero missed this memo. On the count of three, they began to pull on the rope with all their might, and as they strained the tree began to shift, and suddenly—*CRACK!*

Everyone began to run. Well, almost everyone. Our hero hid behind the target tree, covered his ears, closed his eyes, and crouched down dead in the path of the falling tree. The birch bounced and landed less than a foot away from him! The guides were mad, of course, but everyone else was laughing too hard to be angry.

That was one of the many highlights of that ten-day camping trip in the Adirondacks. An observer told our hero, "When we get home, I'm telling the Darwin Awards about this!" And he did.

Reference: Matt Monitto

DARWIN AWARD WINNER: TREE TROUBLE

Not all trees go down peacefully. For example, in 2002 an English tree trimmer decided to save time (again, the notorious time-saving shortcut) and toss the pruned branches of a fir directly into a fire he built near the base of the tree. Predictably, the tree caught fire, putting an end to further time-saving innovations.

Reference: *Darwin Awards 3: Survival of the Fittest*
(Plume, 2004)

At-Risk Survivor: A Killer Serve

Unconfirmed Personal Account
Featuring a student and a tennis ball machine

1990s, SWITZERLAND | During a training lesson on a plush tennis court in Gstaad, a high school student named Elbrus (son of Russian nouveau riche) decided to check out how a tennis ball machine works. Since you're reading this here, you already know the machine was on and working; in other words, shooting balls. Elbrus stuck his nose in front of the machine to inspect that complicated device. Before anyone could react, the next ball struck him right in the face, breaking his nose and knocking him out! It was his lucky day. The machine was *not* set to a maximum power—otherwise it would have killed him.

Reference: Anonymous

At-Risk Survivor: An Un-Fun Whirlwind

Unconfirmed Personal Account
Featuring weather-related machismo

1999, NEVADA | Roofing vacant homes in Sun Valley was the sweetest commute imaginable. I'd wake up, make breakfast, climb a ladder, and *BAM!* I was at work. Two things Sun Valley has: sand and dirt. Front yards: sand and dirt. Backyards: sand and dirt. Between homes: sand and dirt. Guess what the roads are made of. Yeah.

> **I wondered, "Has anyone ever died inside a Dust Devil?"**

Dust was so prevalent that it was constantly being exchanged by dust devils. These tiny tornadoes were always wandering aimlessly about, coming tantalizingly close but never engaging me. You see, I've always been a reckless sort. Personal risk is something I will wager for the prospect of fun. My idea was simple: jump into the first devil of formidable size; not some weak little twister that could only get me dirty. I wanted a contender.

A month passed. My Mexican helper cried out, "Miguel! Look! Look!" And there it was. A monster. My monster, with a thirty-foot footprint, rising hundreds of feet into the air, heading straight for us.

"I'm goin' in!"

To which Joaquin replied, "Nooo, Miguel, noooo." At this point I must tell you, Joaquin was a very reluctant accomplice.

Down the ladder I went, two steps at a time, and as I ran closer and heard the roar I must say I had second thoughts. But stupidity got the best of me, so eager was I to interact with this behemoth. In I rushed.

Instantly all the air was sucked out of my lungs. My eyes were filled with high-velocity sand and what little breath I could draw was just detritus from the tornado. As the twister pulled me toward its center, the feeling of being planted firmly on the ground was diminishing, and something wanted my body to spin.

My idea was simple: jump into the first devil of formidable size.

The violence was so intense that I wondered to myself, "Could one of these kill someone? Has anyone ever *died* inside a dust devil?" When it finally released me, I went down onto my hands and knees, choking and gagging, and kissed the ground. Joaquin rushed to my side and frantically communicated that he thought I was a goner. To which I gasped, "I'd like to do that again."

Joaquin just shook his head and muttered, *"Estupido."*

Reference: Anonymous

From dust we came, and to dust we shall return.
—Ecclesiastes 3:20

At-Risk Survivor: Medieval Mayhem

Unconfirmed Personal Account
Featuring explosions, weather, and women

AUGUST (VARIOUS YEARS), PENNSYLVANIA | Every summer, the Society for Creative Anachronism holds a two-week-long "war" in a cornfield in Pennsylvania. The Darwin Awards team loves SCA members for their welcoming enthusiasm and their passion for medieval history and arts both fine and martial. But in any large organization, there are always a few outliers. And at an event the size of Pennsic, which attracts over ten thousand attendees from around the world, there are bound to be some potential Darwin Award winners running around. For example:

Fighters have two neurons— one is lost and the other is out looking for it.

A knight fell "dead" (i.e., passed out) on the battlefield after a minor body blow. When he came to, he revealed that his appendix had been removed just last weekend, and he was still stapled shut from surgery. Ladies, protect your fighters! Hide your knight's helmet if he intends to endanger himself.

A woman was taken to the camp's medical facility with heat exhaustion verging on heat stroke. Attempts to lower her temperature failed. Finally the EMTs removed her clothing to apply ice. Beneath her elaborate historic dress, they found that she was wrapped neck to ankles in plastic wrap, in order to lose weight. Removing the plastic wrap brought her temperature under control. Remember: Your date wants to stroke *you*, not plastic!

When the damp weather made it hard to get a campfire started, a knight suggested using a capful of white gas. His squire heard "cupful" and poured on two. The fumes became a situation. The knight, a real-life munitions expert, said, "We've got to burn it to defuse it!" He lit a piece of

> **The munitions expert said, "We've got to burn it to defuse it!"**

paper and kicked it into the pit. *WHOOMPH!* A fourteen-foot column of white-hot fire was the result. An actor in a nearby play glanced offstage, did a double-take, and hollered, "Fire!" to the crowded theater. The mushroom cloud could be seen a mile away. The squire was restricted from using accelerants henceforth.

Reference: Wendy "Darwin" Northcutt

Reader Comment

"Three reasons to love the SCA!"

SCIENCE INTERLUDE
BATTY BEHAVIOR

By Cassandra Brooks

Fellatio is surprisingly rare in the animal kingdom. Humans do it, of course—though it's still illegal in some states. And bonobo chimps, our close African ape relatives, do it—though really, what won't they do? But in the wee hours of the night, researchers happened upon wild female *fruit bats* regularly performing fellatio during mating.

Researchers in China were studying the short-nosed fruit bat, *Cynopterus sphinx,* native to Southeast Asia. As expected, males built tent nests out of fan palms and began to court friendly females. Once a female was inside the nest, the couple groomed each other, a courtship behavior common in many animals. The male initiated intercourse—no surprises there—but then, to the researchers' astonishment, the lady bat bent down and began to fellate her mate!

Was it just a few bats treading on the wild side? After witnessing this act in the wild, the researchers observed captive animals. Incredibly, 70 percent of the female bats performed fellatio—and with great rewards. Frisky females received sex for twice as long, doubling intercourse time from two minutes to more than four! And the males never withdrew while the lady was providing extra stimulation.

Is this batty behavior really so rare and strange? Unfortunately the literature doesn't say. You won't find the answer in any Google Scholar search. Traditional science is reluctant to study sex, but Bruce Bagemihl, an *independent* scholar and author, is not a traditional scientist.

Bagemihl scoured the scientific literature for data left out of the main findings and interviewed researchers to uncover data that was absent from the literature altogether. His book, based on ten years of avid research, rocked the reproductive biology world. *Biological Exuberance: Animal Sexuality and Natural Diversity* revealed that nonbreeding behavior is common in hundreds of animals. From sheep to vampire bats, 470 species have been observed engaged in masturbation, fellatio, homosexuality, or other nonbreeding sexual behavior. In contrast to the short-nosed fruit bats, however, most instances were same-sex encounters or experimentation between playful juveniles, and not a regular part of adult heterosexual coupling.

Nonreproductive sex raises questions—as well as eyebrows—especially if it is commonplace. According to Darwinian evolution theory, animals are instruments for gene propagation, so why waste energy on pointless sexual pursuits? Try as one might, it is difficult to ascribe any direct evolutionary benefit to "batty behavior." But if there is no reproductive benefit, why is kinky sex so popular?

Primate experience might provide some insight. In the majority of human matings, there is no ostensible tie with reproduction. We have no cues to show we are ovulating, so we do it throughout a woman's reproductive cycle, we do it long after we cease being fertile, and we do it all for pleasure. Bonobos aren't much different. Of their sexual liaisons, 75 percent happen when the females are not fertile, lending credence to the idea that sex is partly driven by pleasure. In fact, some bold researchers argue that pleasure itself provides a huge incentive to engage in sex frequently (well, *duh*) and the more often an animal has sex, the greater the chance that a bun is rising in the oven.

Well and good for primates, but why do *female fruit bats* spend their precious time performing fellatio? Maybe bats are doing it for fun, and maybe not. There might be more practical reasons for their oral obsession. The authors speculate that fellatio might prolong mating by maintaining the erection and increasing lubrication, which in turn may facilitate sperm transport. Longer mating also keeps the male occupied and away from rival ladies. And hygiene may play a role—saliva has antimicrobial properties and may protect against diseases. Some bat species lick themselves postcoitus, presumably for this reason.

There are also less obvious benefits beyond enhancing reproduction. Consider those playful bonobo chimps, who will purportedly have intimate relations regardless of age, gender, location, or time. Research suggests that their "loose" behavior reduces social tensions, enhances bonding, and resolves conflicts in their large, close community. Fondling a friend helps a bonobo gain access to resources ("I like your banana and I'm willing to give you fellatio for it") or turn an enemy into an ally. This indirectly improves reproductive success.

Whether frisky fruit bats are fellating for social leverage, for fun, or for fecundity remains unclear.

But it does provide a thought-provoking example of nonbreeding behavior in animals, and might encourage open-mindedness about the issue. Scientists will have to keep spying—in the middle of the night and in strange places—to uncover the diversity and meaning of it all. Until then, let the festivities continue.

FURTHER READING:

Bruce Bagemihl, *Biological Exuberance: Animal Homosexuality and Natural Diversity* (New York: St. Martin's Press, 1999), 768.

Frans De Waal, *Bonobo: The Forgotten Ape* (Berkeley: University of California Press, 1997), 200.

Jared Diamond, *Why Is Sex Fun?: The Evolution of Human Sexuality* (New York: Basic Books, 1997), 176.

M. Tan, G. Jones, G. Zhu, J. Ye, T. Hong, et al., "Fellatio by Fruit Bats Prolongs Copulation Time," PLoS ONE 4 (2009), 10, http://www.plosone.org/article/info%3Adoi%2F10.1371%2Fjournal.pone.0007595

CHAPTER 1

DOUBLE DARWINS! TWICE AS NICE

"Now, tell me these stories don't make you feel superior!"
—typical Fan mail

Double trouble, double delight, double dipping in the gene pool. Six astounding and rare Double Darwins and At-Risk Survivors, from a chaste cleric to a criminal caper, from upping the ante on fun to raising the stakes on a feud . . . Are you willing to risk it all and *double down?*

Padre Baloneiro—Balloon Priest • Double Parking • Crushing Debt • Low-Flying Drunks • Putting the Pain in Propane • Agua Ski Calamity

Adelir Antonio, fifty-one, was not so lucky.

Double Darwin Award Winner:
Padre Baloneiro—Balloon Priest

Confirmed by Darwin
Featuring helium, faith, and a priest!

Priest Visits Boss

20 APRIL 2008, ATLANTIC OCEAN A Catholic priest's audacious attempt to set a world record for clustered balloon flight succeeded, he set a record beyond his wildest dreams . . . The priest literally ascended to heaven on a host of helium party balloons, paying homage to Lawn Chair Larry's aerial adventure. In 1982, Larry Walters attached forty-five huge weather balloons to his lawn chair, packed a picnic lunch, and cut the tether—but instead of drifting above Los Angeles's backyard "babescape" as planned, he was rocketed into LAX air traffic lanes by the tremendous lift of the balloons. Astoundingly, Larry survived the flight, inspiring the movies *Deckchair Danny, Up!* and Father Adelir Antonio, fifty-one.

> Hot air balloons are actually maneuverable, by altering altitude. The wind direction tends to change as one ascends, generally toward the right in the Northern Hemisphere. A skillful pilot uses altitude adjustments to shift the downwind track. By comparison, a mass of party balloons is completely at the mercy of the wind.

This priest's audacious attempt to set a world record (currently, nineteen hours) for clustered balloon flight was dreamed up to publicize his plan to build spiritual rest stops for truckers. More rest stops are sorely needed, as sure as sore bums need rest. But as truckers know, sitting put for nineteen hours is no trivial matter, even in the comfort of a decked-out lawn chair.

The priest did take numerous precautions: wearing a survival suit; packing a buoyant chair, a satellite phone, and GPS. However, the late A.A. made a fatal mistake. He did not learn how to use one important safety feature: the GPS.

Once he was well aloft the wind changed, as winds do, and he was blown inexorably toward open sea. He could have parachuted to safety while over land *but chose not to.* When the voyager was perilously lost at sea, he finally phoned for help—but rescuers were unable to determine his location, since he could not use his GPS. He struggled with the unit as the cell phone batteries dwindled and died.

Instead of a GPS, the priest let God be his guide.

Over the next few weeks, bits of balloons began appearing on mountains and beaches—indications that God had guided him straight to heaven! Ultimately the priest's body surfaced, confirming that he had indeed "paid a visit to the boss."

The kicker? It's a Double Darwin. Catholic priests take vows of celibacy and *voluntarily remove themselves* from the gene pool. The entire group earns a mass Darwin Award, so . . . Father Antonio wins twice!

Reference: globo.com, *Sydney Morning Herald*, Associated Press, and numerous others

Reader Comments

"Don't get carried away."

"Chairway to Heaven."

"Shows the danger of relying on GPS."

"See what happens when you swear off women?"

"There but for the grace of . . ."

"One-way ticket to paradise."

"To heaven—or bust!"

"There but for the grace of Tecumseh . . ."

"God's will be done!"

SCIENCE SOAPBOX: REST STOPS ARE NECESSARY AND GOOD

Father Adelir Antonio gave his life for a worthy cause: To halt the closure of roadside rest stops, which are urgently needed in areas with long stretches of freeway that lack commercial services. Rest stops provide a much-needed break for weary drivers, and are especially needed by truckers who transport food and merchandise across the country. They cost little to maintain and increase public safety. The closure of rest stops in Brazil was blasted by the media as unnecessary, harmful, and bad policy. Father Adelir gave his life for a laudable goal. He is a brave and shining example of the good done by Catholic clergy.

BALLOON HOAX

On October 15, 2009, the distraught parents of a six-year-old reported that their child was possibly adrift aboard a huge, homemade helium balloon that they had launched from their lawn. The silver, flying saucer–shaped dirigible was tracked by National Guard helicopters and local police as it drifted across Colorado for sixty miles. Planes were rerouted around the object's flight path and Denver International Airport was briefly shut down. The balloon finally landed after a two-hour flight—but the child was not on board.

Fearing that the youth had fallen from the balloon, authorities began a comprehensive manhunt of the entire area beneath its flight path. Worldwide media followed the spectacle, which culminated hours later with the anticlimactic discovery that the child had been hiding at home the entire time!

Suspicions soon arose that the incident was a hoax and publicity stunt, particularly following a family interview by Wolf Blitzer on *Larry King Live*. The youngster, when asked the reason for hiding, turned to Dad and blurted out, "You guys said that, um, we did this for the show." The family had twice been featured in a reality TV show, and may have been eager for a third run.

Two months later, Dad pleaded guilty to "attempting to influence a public servant" and was sentenced to ninety days in jail and fined $36,000; Mom was sentenced to twenty weekend days in jail.

Reference: Condensed from Wikipedia.org

Double Darwin Award Winner: Double Parking

Confirmed by Darwin

Featuring macho gunmen

10 DECEMBER 2009, PHILIPPINES | This small island nation has already produced several of the most illustrious Darwin Award winners. In 1999, National Bureau of Investigation agents snuffed their candles when they sneaked a smoke in a room full of seized explosives. In 2000, an airplane hijacker robbed passengers then bailed out with an untested homemade parachute. Talk about drop-dead funny! Now the Philippines have produced that rare oddity, the Double Darwin Award.

We begin with Francisco C. and Ronaldo C., two businessmen who own restaurants adjacent to each other on Apacible Boulevard in Batangas. One has partially blocked the door to the other's establishment, and this does not sit well. Tempers erupt. Heated words are exchanged; a fistfight breaks out! But bystanders pacify the fighters, and the situation is defused.

Or is it? Each man retreats to his respective car, pulls out a gun, and shoots the other—killing both combatants. Francisco, forty-one, suffered two bullet wounds to his chest; Ronaldo, thirty-nine, was shot once beneath his arm. Francisco and Ronaldo: Two enemies brought together in death—much to their own chagrin.

Reference: abs-cbnnews.com

Double Darwin Award Winner: Crushing Debt

Confirmed by Darwin

Featuring criminals, explosions, and a double Darwin!

26 SEPTEMBER 2009, BELGIUM | The city of Dinant is the backdrop for this rare Double Darwin Award. Two bank robbers attempting to make a sizeable withdrawal from an ATM died when they *overestimated* the quantity of dynamite needed for the explosion. The blast demolished the ATM, and the entire building the bank was housed in. Nobody else was in the building at the time of the attack.

Two bank robbers *overestimated* the quantity of dynamite needed to crack the ATM.

Robber #1 was rushed to the hospital with severe skull trauma; he died shortly after arrival. Investigators initially believed that his accomplice had managed a getaway, but the second bungler's body was excavated from the debris twelve hours later.

Would-be Robbers 1 and 2 weren't exactly impoverished—their getaway car was a BMW.

Reference: *Le Soir*—lesoir.be, *De Standaard*—standaard.be, deredactie.be, nu.nl, demorgen.be

Reader Comments

"Dynamite: not for everything."

"Less is certainly more."

"They certainly thought BIG."

"A debit card would have been safer."

"They really blew it . . ."

WEIRD SCIENCE: DARWINTUNES

An Evolutionary Idea in Music.

Using an "evolutionary algorithm" and the ears of the general public, DarwinTunes has been evolving a four-bar loop that began as a primordial auditory soup. After two-hundred-plus generations, the musical track is sounding pretty good. Project leaders recently upped the maximum genome size, and they seek your help.

The DarwinTunes Experiment Needs You!

www.darwintunes.org

Evolve the Music.

Double Darwin Award Winner: Low-Flying Drunks

Unconfirmed

Featuring airplanes, alcohol, and a double Darwin!

1996, CANADA | Sleeping residents of Chilliwack were awakened early one morning by the sound of a small aircraft flying lower than usual. The engine sounded like a mosquito, zooming too close too quick, then veering away. What the bleep was going on?

During a bout of heavy drinking that lasted into the wee hours of the morning, two future Darwin Award winners had realized that although neither one had a pilot's license nor flight training, they nevertheless knew all they needed to know to pilot an aircraft. Furthermore, one of the gentlemen worked at the small local airport and had access to the tarmac.

They drew the obvious conclusion and decided to take a plane for a drunken joyride over the city. They invited two females along for the ride; fortunately the level-headed ladies declined.

From idea to execution, the plan evolved quickly. The airport employee unlocked locked gates; once on the tarmac, the two then managed to break into a small plane, taxi to the runway, and get it off the ground and into the sky. They buzzed around in the dark, skimming above the roofs of the houses, and no doubt exchanging a few gleeful high-fives. This random aerial activity went on for an extended period of time.

Eventually their bladders began to complain, but they no longer remembered how to find the airport.

Disoriented, they attempted to land on the grassy median between east- and westbound lanes of the Trans-Canada Highway and *almost* made it under the electrical wires that cross the median.

Where these wires were concerned, fate was not kind.

The tail of the aircraft clipped the wires and the plane took a nose-dive. Instead of making a soft landing on the grassy verge, it greeted the ground with enthusiasm, killing both occupants. Only then were the sleepy Chilliwack residents able to return to their interrupted dreams.

Reference: *Chilliwack Progress* newspaper, edition unknown.

At-Risk Survivors:
Putting the Pain in Propane

Confirmed by Reliable Eyewitness
Featuring alcohol, fire, gas, and explosions!

"You gotta see this."

DECEMBER 2008, FLORIDA | An engine company sent a request for the Jacksonville Fire and Rescue Department to extinguish a routine trash fire. The District Chief for the fire department said, "The lieutenant said, '*You gotta see this.*'" Everyone wanted to share a piece of the action. An intoxicated group of men had decided that throwing paint cans into their fifty-five-gallon drum fire was fun, but not fun enough. They escalated the excitement by tossing in not one, but three twenty-pound propane cylinders.

Everyone wanted to share a piece of the action.

The fun went south when one cylinder violently vented toward an unfortunate reveler. We cannot reveal the patient's name due to HIPAA laws, but he was transported to a burn unit for attention to his "party favors." The gene pool is still at risk from these rocket scientists, as the close call was not fatal.

Reference: A medic acting as District Chief in the incident

According to the District Chief, partially empty propane cylinders are actually more dangerous than full ones because they cannot absorb as much heat prior to venting or exploding.

At-Risk Survivors:
Agua Ski Calamity

Unconfirmed Personal Account

Featuring water, alcohol, do-it-yourself ingenuity, and a boat

29 DECEMBER 2009, MEXICO | Sun, sea, sand, well-built hombres in small bathing suits, tropical drinks—Mazatlán is everything you could wish for on a long No-Freakin'-Snow! winter holiday. Boats are rented, sunscreen slathered on, rum-related judgment-impairing drinks poured, what could possibly go sideways?

Enter Oscar, thirty-four, Scooter, twenty-two, and their fifty-eight-year-old mom, Taffy. Their favorite warm-weather activity is water skiing, especially after the consumption of two or three drinks with paper umbrellas. If the Olympics makes Near-Death Experience a medal event, these three will clean up.

The lack of a tow rope vexed the colorful trio until one child of Bacchus recruited the others to execute a plan to MAKE TOW ROPE so they could go skiing. The ingredients for this makeshift replacement were deep-sea fishing line, the patience to braid fifty yards of doom–in-the-making, and a handle to affix to the rope. Taffy's always up for sacrificing her bikini top for a good cause, so that was the tow rope handle.

It was like watching a train wreck unfold. The boat engine revved, Taffy jumped in, Leo was at the wheel. Scooter put on the water skis, bobbed into position, and shouted, "Hit it!" The boat reached warp nine before the braided line suffered what NASA would call a catastrophic failure, snapping in half somewhere along its length, coming apart at the bikini handle, the hitch, and Poseidon only knows where else.

Out-of-control Scooter was sent flying over a low boat ramp and into the open hold of a fishing boat. A highly irate Mexican fisherman threw him and his skis back overboard. Taffy got spanked with fishing line lashes across her back, and Leo narrowly missed plowing into a tourist boat due to the combination of excess speed and sudden loss of drag.

Turns out, tickets for "disturbing the peace" and "public drunkenness" add up to $130 in fines and a good scolding from the judge, who pointed out the obvious at length: This could have been tragic, Scooter could have broken his neck, and Leo could have sunk a tourist boat that was chock-full of little kids.

As for me, this year I'm gonna stay home and shovel the driveway.

Reference: blrqul of Ogden, Utah

CHAPTER 0

FAQ: You Ask, We Tell

What are the Darwin Awards? • Who can win one? What are the rules? • Is there an actual, physical Darwin Award? • Are any winners alive? • Where do you get your stories? • How do you confirm the stories? • Have you ever been wrong? • How many submissions do you get? • Are the winners decided by vote? • Why aren't these buckets of testosterone on your list? • Who writes the great Science essays? • Why are Science essays in a humor book? • What is the history of this dubious distinction? • The Darwin Awards are written by . . . a woman!? • What do the families think? • I have kids. Am I safe? • Are humans really evolving? • Isn't there something beautiful about moronic creativity? • Why so many men? • Why do we laugh at death? • What inspired you to do this? • What are your aspirations? • How many stories? How many books? How many more? • Are you making a movie, musical, or TV show? • Do you drive while using a cell phone? • What were those Five (5) Rules, again?

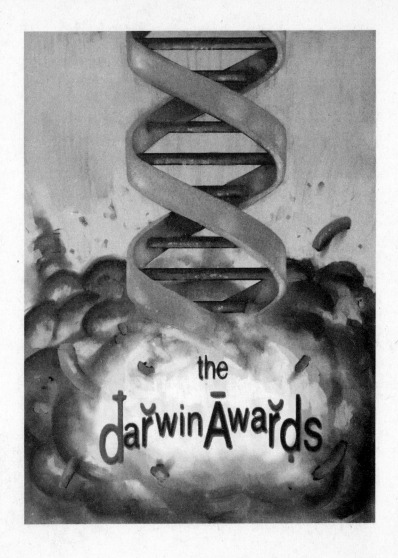

FAQ: What are the Darwin Awards?

Darwin Awards: A Chronicle of Enterprising Demises

Heroic service to humanity deserves recognition and respect. To that end, we have created the Darwin Award, named for evolutionary theorist Charles Darwin, to honor those who willingly sacrifice their own lives to the process of natural selection. The Darwin Awards recognize individuals who ensure the long-term survival of the human race by removing themselves from it in a sublimely idiotic fashion, thereby ensuring that future generations are descended from one less idiot.

Darwin Awards: Improving the Human Race One Idiot at a Time
This tongue-in-cheek award is based on the premise that the human species is still evolving, and we see this every time someone manages to kill himself in a really clueless way. An unfortunate loss to be sure, but observe that the human race just got *smarter* by one idiot. Charles Darwin would call that evolution.

> Here's a toast to you, sir, for your noble self-sacrifice.
>
> —Wendy

The Darwin Awards are not legends. They are true, and that is what makes them so fascinating.

FAQ: Who can win one?
What are the rules?

Wendy debated philosophy with readers and fans concerning the merits of specific nominees such as wrestler Owen Hart and the Shaker cult that forbade sex, and philosophical concerns such as identical twins, age, inbreeding, etc. These conversations distilled down to Five Simple Rules:

1. Death.
2. Excellence.
3. Self-selection.
4. Maturity.
5. Veracity.

To win a Darwin Award, an *adult* must eliminate *himself* from the *gene pool* in an *astonishingly* stupid way that is verifiably *true*.

1. *Death: Out of the gene pool!*
   The winner proves he is a reproductive dead end by rendering himself deceased—or, more happily, alive though incapable of reproducing. Sheer stupidity is not enough. If someone, some-where, somehow manages to survive an incredibly stupid feat, those genes ipso facto have something to offer in the way of luck, agility, or stamina—and therefore the perpetrator is not eligible for a Darwin Award.

2. *Excellence.*
   The true Darwin Award winner exhibits a staggering lack of judg-

ment. The final fatal act is of truly phenomenal, pots-of-gold magnitude, like playing with electric wires while standing in the Jacuzzi (p. 179). The Darwin Award winner overlooks risks that are seemingly *impossible* to overlook. Shooting at dynamite (p. 146), anchoring your boat with a bomb (p. 151), surfing during a hurricane (p. 223)... all you can say is, *"What were they thinking?"*

3. *Self-selection: The candidate causes his own demise.*
   Nobody can give you a Darwin Award. You must earn it yourself by showing self-evident ineptitude for survival. A hiker hit by a falling tree is merely a victim of circumstance. But if you *roped that tree* and pulled it over on yourself... you are a candidate for a Darwin Award. (p. 232)

   If you intentionally try to win, you are disqualified. We wish to discourage risk-taking behavior, whereas giving publicity to people attempting foolhardy stunts will only encourage them. Most extreme sports accidents are also rejected, because that person made an intentional choice that the risk was worth the reward. *Not every action that is risky, is stupid.*

4. *Maturity:* Those who are young or lack intellect *are not eligible.*

   Those who lack maturity of age or intellect *are not eligible* for an Award. A child does not possess sufficient experience to make life-or-death decisions nor are juvenile neurons fully wired, so the responsibility for the child's safety resides with his guardians. *Age sixteen is our rule of thumb.* Some readers (particularly young adults) argue that children *should* be

THIS BOOK features both Darwin Awards and At-Risk Survivors.

At-Risk Survivors are just that: People who narrowly escaped a near-death experience. Many are personal accounts—explained by *the self-same idiot who planned and survived it*—which certainly serve as sobering tales!

eligible to win, but frankly, we just don't think the death of a youth is funny. Similarly the downfall of a person with mental handicaps (such as age-related cognitive impairment) is not amusing. We prefer to laugh at those who should have seen it coming.

5. *Veracity: The event is true.*
Truth is stranger—and funnier—than fiction. We rely on reputable news organizations, responsible eyewitnesses (emergency responders, utility company employees, monks), and whenever possible, multiple independent sources. We also recommend the use of a bullshit radar and a quick reality check at Snopes or Google.

FAQ: Is there an actual, physical Darwin Award?

It would be great if there was an actual Darwin Award! But who would we give it to? And what would it be? A bust of Charles Darwin? A herd of dodo birds? A small, personalized tombstone? A beagle? A disintegrating strand of DNA? Someday there will be an actual, physical Darwin Award that you can give to a boneheaded friend as a warning. Until then, simply appreciate the abstract beauty of the ethereal Darwin Award.

FAQ: Are any winners alive?

Yes, an occasional foolish mortal accepts the prize in person. You see, Darwin Award winners are (*whistle*) out of the gene pool—but not necessarily dead! The lucky few who survive amorous encounters with a vacuum cleaner, a glass vase (p. 83, "SINGLE BUD VASE"), a porcupine or park bench (p. 79, "BENCH PRESS")— examples chosen at random—these "lucky" few lose their ability to procreate and are dead to the next generation, yet alive to collect the trophy.

We also chronicle those who deserve honorable mentions for surviving not-quite-fatal incidents—through no fault of their own. At-Risk Survivors stop short of making the ultimate sacrifice but embody the valiant and creative spirit of a true Darwin Award contender.

Don't stand too close to an At-Risk Survivor!

FAQ: Where do you get your stories?

From you!

Every Darwin Award begins as a website submission. Nominations come from around the world, and moderators review the latest self-annihilations while chanting the Rules: "Death. Excellence. Self-selection. Maturity. Veracity."

Readers rate the Slush stories on a 1–10 scale, and we review those with the highest vote, referring to the Five Rules, moderator comments, and our own intuition when deciding if a story should make the cut. Five to ten sub-

Potential Darwin Award? At-Risk Survivor?
The best submissions land in the Slush Pile:
www.DarwinAwards.com/slush

missions per month are deemed ludicrous enough to become a Darwin Award. Assisted by snarky reader comments, Wendy turns dry news reports into amusing (but factual) vignettes, and they go forth into the public arena.

But that's not the end of the process! Actually it's a new beginning.* The Darwin Awards website reaches one million visitors each month, and on average, each story is read twenty thousand times a month! With this vast audience, we hear about mistakes. Corrections, confirmations, and snarky comments are added to the stories continually. They are updated and sometimes disqualified based on community comments.

The stories herein have been scrutinized and vetted, and they are accurate to the best of our knowledge at press time. But due to the dynamic processes described above, they are *not guaranteed* to be entirely accurate. They are a snapshot of the state of human evolution at the time of this writing.

As you read the tales we bring you, keep in mind the care with which each gem was culled from dozens of competitors and honed to its current form. (:

---

* Sounds like a rehab program: "New Beginnings."

FAQ: How do you confirm the stories?

The words *Confirmed by Darwin* indicate that a story is backed up by reputable media sources, plausible eyewitnesses such as emergency responders, or multiple independent eyewitness accounts. You can find the original reports on the Darwin Awards website, linked from the bottom of each story's webpage.

All the stories are believed to be true. We may gloss over grimy bits and change the names of survivors, but we include every detail about the perpetrator, his motivation, and his methods. Sometimes supporting documentation is insufficient to confirm. Instead of tossing away a perfectly good cautionary tale, we label it UNCONFIRMED and seek additional verification. Often—surprisingly often—readers e-mail the details and confirmation needed.

If you know important facts, *please contact us!*
www.DarwinAwards.com/book/contact

In the *At-Risk Survivor* stories, be aware that we do change names and obscure details in order to provide a measure of anonymity for the innocent—and for that matter, the guilty.

FAQ: Have you ever been wrong?

Yes! Sometimes, spectacularly wrong.

Once upon a time, a man wanted to know what it feels like to be shot with cigarette butts. He loaded an old-fashioned muzzle-loader—persuaded a friend to turn the ciggie-gun on him—and was killed by *three butts to the heart!* We featured this numbingly ridiculous story in 2001, labeling it CONFIRMED BY DARWIN, and reveled in witticisms like "Smoking Kills" and "Cigarettes Proved Deadly." Seven years later, *MythBusters* asked us to provide our sources—and finding them missing or suspicious, we declared, IT'S A HOAX, A LEGEND, COMPLETELY FABRICATED. But in 2010, e-mail from a family friend citing media references, names, and Facebook accounts, reconvinced us that the poor man was indeed killed by cigarette butts!

> For more details on The Smoking Gun, visit
> www.DarwinAwards.com/book/cigarette

Yes, we have been wrong and wronger, more than once and more than twice. But we aren't afraid to say we were wrong. That's why you can trust us. We continually **correct errors** and update the stories with new information, and you can always find the latest scoop on the Darwin Awards website.

The Darwin Awards are not legends. They are true, and that is what makes them so funny.

FAQ: How many submissions do you get?

Two hundred to four hundred submissions per month. A particularly inspirational story might be submitted hundreds of times. A recent avalanche was in April 2008, when a priest went aloft in a lawn chair tethered to hundreds of helium party balloons—and that was the last we saw of him for many months.

FAQ: Are the winners decided by vote?

If votes were all that mattered, you would see more stories about poop and procreation. Put one or both of these in a story, and its score goes up. Grotesque stories also get a boost. We let the popular vote *guide* our preference—but not *rule* it.

Your vote has the most influence in choosing the best of the Slush, pointing out stories that need more polish, and picking the annual Winners.

Case example: Wendy loved a story that kept getting low votes. A Californian was working on a laptop *while driving;* he drifted over the centerline and was killed. Ha-ha! Ha? Bafflingly unpopular. She rewrote the story four times, trying to convey the humor, but still its score remained low. Minor injuries were suffered by the innocent; that can kill a nomination. In the end, she heeded your votes and removed it from consideration.

FAQ: Why aren't *these* buckets of testosterone on your list?

We often get enthusiastic pointers to evolution-about-to-happen, for example, crocodile-baiting teenage boys. When young men are being stupid just to garner attention, additional publicity will feed into and actually promote risk-taking. We draw the line at *encouraging* dangerous stupidity! But certainly croc-baiters (and so forth) are walking into the maw of natural selection.

> "Croc-baiters are walking into the maw of natural selection."

FAQ: Who writes the great Science essays?

The essays in this book were written by graduates of the science writing program at the University of California, Santa Cruz. This program has produced professional science writers since 1981. If you read major science magazines, go to science museums and aquaria, or listen to NPR, you've seen and heard their work. The essays in this book were written by Slugs, as the alumni of UCSC call themselves, and we are honored to share their exceptional work with you.

FAQ: *Why* are there Science essays in a humor book?

Wendy says, "I'm a Scientist! I live and breathe science." The Darwin Awards are based on the scientific premise that humans are evolving. A large portion of our readers are college students, or first heard about the Darwin Awards whilst in college. The Science essays are relevant—often explaining advanced evolutionary concepts—and keep Scientist Wendy interested in her job. "Charles Darwin would be disappointed if I focused only on humor and failed to contribute to scientific knowledge," says Wendy.

FAQ: What is the history of this dubious distinction?

In 1993, Wendy began writing Darwin Award vignettes and gathering a wide audience by sending regular newsletters, encouraging submissions, and facilitating discussions and voting. Her hobby became a consuming passion, as the fans grew from hundreds to thousands, tens of thousands, millions . . .

Thanks to Wendy's tireless efforts, today a Darwin Award is a worldwide symbol of stupidity.

Wendy writes the stories, but the Darwin Awards belong to all of us. The heart and soul of the Darwin Awards is our community. *All* the stories are available on the website, updated with facts, comments, and quips from readers. The Darwin Awards grows with your guidance. We prune stories when you convince us our judgment is flawed—if the deceased was the victim of a bizarre accident rather than his own bizarre judgment—or more subtle points such as whether the person is mentally incompetent (for example, "Saw It Coming!" p. 202).

Wendy's goal is to maintain this network of people and keep this cultural icon true to its origins.

When Wendy began chronicling the Darwin Awards, there were

only a few in existence. The first use of the term "Darwin Awards" is obscure. Usenet archives contains an August 1985 mention of the fellow crushed beneath a Coke machine while he was trying to shake loose a free can—true story! Five years later, an urban legend surfaced about a man who strapped a JATO rocket to his Chevy, turning it into a doomed aircraft. Wendy took over the helm of the Beagle and began writing the Darwin Awards in 1993; since then, *thousands of people have aspired to win a Darwin Award*—nine thousand submissions in the last three years alone.

FAQ: The Darwin Awards are written by . . . a woman!?

Wendy writes the stories, but the heart and soul of the Darwin Awards is our community. We maintain a vibrant network of contributors and keep this cultural icon connected to its community.

Yes, Wendy is a woman. That makes the Darwin Awards a kinder, gentler place. She deals with flames sympathetically. She says NO! to racial stereotypes and just-plain-mean submissions. When community or family complain, she listens respectfully to their point of view. These discussions lead to facts being corrected; sometimes the story is removed, other times the family takes solace from knowing that their loss is at least a "safety lesson" to help others avoid the same mistake.

FAQ: What do the families think?

If a family writes to us, we take their concerns seriously. Sometimes we remove the story. We don't want to cause anyone pain. Sometimes the family realizes that their loss has a little more meaning if it serves as a cautionary tale that might save someone else's life. Often they even confide prior foolhardy things that the winner did.

Like an Irish wake, it can be healing to laugh while you grieve. That's human nature.

Sometimes families write to share a memory. From a recent email:

"Many years ago my two uncles started roughhousing at our Christmas gathering. At one point Uncle Frank picked up Uncle John by the heels, lost his grip, and dropped Uncle John on his head. It was all right because John was a state supreme court justice and there for life. The other uncle is, I am sure, in your archive. The one about the skydiving photographer who forgot to put on a chute . . ."

Where's the Shoot? Where's the Chute?
http://darwinawards.com/darwin/darwin1994-12.html

FAQ: I have kids. Am I safe?

You passed along your genes. You're safe!

The broader question is whether a person with offspring has opted out of a Darwin Award. Our community engages in inconclusive discussions about what it means to be *out of the gene pool*. What if the winner has already reproduced? Obviously a winner with no kids is *more* "out of the gene pool" than one who leaves behind several ankle biters, so shouldn't rug rats rule you out?

What about a vow of celibacy, is that an automatic win? What if the nominee has an identical twin, and his DNA is still running around trying to reproduce? How about old people who aren't able to have any (more) kids—are the elderly disqualified? And the whole topic of cryogenics is troubling. Unbeknownst to us, have so-called winners left frozen sperm and eggs laying around? If cloning humans becomes feasible (it is already *possible*), Darwin Awards might cease to exist!

These questions are vexing. And the answers . . . we just don't know. The rule of thumb is, if you no longer have the physical wherewithal to breed with a mate on a desert island, *you* are out of the gene pool.

FAQ: Are humans really evolving?

Yes! Although technological advances have extended the average lifespan, the mechanism of evolution still applies: (1) a species must show variation; (2) that variation must be inheritable; (3) not all members of the population survive to reproduce; but (4) the inherited characteristics of some members make them more likely to do so. Not only are humans still evolving, we are doing it faster than ever before. There is solid evidence that human evolution has accelerated dramatically in the past ten thousand years.*

> "Stupidity is the only universal capital crime . . .
>   and execution is carried out automatically."
> —Robert Heinlein
> *Time Enough for Love*

"Survival of the fittest" alters a species gradually—over thousands of generations—or quickly when it eliminates the dodo who does

---

* In fact, humans are evolving faster than ever before.
  For more on human evolution, read Rapid Evolution, p. 211.

not avoid the club. It eliminates with equal ease the bird that flies into a window and the driver who weaves around the freeway yakking on a phone. *Without a doubt, humans are "really" evolving.* We won't recognize ourselves in a hundred thousand years.

But whether the Darwin Awards represent human evolution is less clear. Is there a set of genes that causes a man to kite board during a hurricane (p. 223) or a woman to chase a feather (p. 105) off a cliff? Do chromosomes play a role in the decision to jump into a dust devil? (p. 236) These actions do not appear to have a direct genetic link.

Here at Darwin Central, all we know is that a person who does not survive through his own acts is *manifestly* less fit than the rest of us. Said genes are *ipso facto* gone from the future, and we can only hope there *is* a genetic link because that means the next generation will see fewer people shooting stashes of dynamite, (p. 146) staging risky accidents for insurance (p. 123), or anchoring boats with ordnance (p. 151).

FAQ: Isn't there something beautiful about moronic creativity?

Yes, there is indeed a poetic beauty here. The well-planned Darwin Award can illustrate the creativity and genius that distinguishes us from less adaptable species. The same innovative spirit that causes the downfall of a Darwin Award winner is also responsible for the social and scientific advances that make the human race great. Cheese, flight, electricity, and small businesses are some of the benefits to having risk takers living (and dying) among us.

FAQ: Why so many men?

"Is a feminist conspiracy at work in the selection of the candidates?"

—Concerned Reader

Nearly all of the submissions for this ignominious Award are on behalf of male perps. Ten percent or fewer are female, and of those 10 percent, more are likely to be At-Risk Survivors. Pure observation leads us to conclude that males are risk takers and driven to daring feats. It's a gender difference. Get over it.

FAQ: Why do we laugh about death?

Laughter helps us cope with tragedy.

Wendy says, "I see a little of myself in every story. As one of the world's biggest klutzes my final hour will likely find me clutching a Darwin Award. If so, I hope my family and friends will laugh through their tears and say, *That's just like Wendy. Oh, she was such an idiot!*

Why are the Darwin Awards funny? Readers wax eloquent on the subject:

"Eventually you die. That's life. And fifty years later you die again because everybody has forgotten you. But if your exit is newsworthy, there's a good chance you will be remembered within your own family, at least. The Darwin Award winners of today will have their memories cherished longer, by more people, than those who die peacefully in bed."

"Want to feel like a genius? Next time you feel foolish or incompetent, read a few and you will soon realize how brilliant you really are compared to the morons out there."

"Just makes you feel better about your own intelligence."

"One truly admires those individuals whose efforts at immortality lift the veil of depression from the rest of us mortals stuck on this rock."

"You think you've got troubles?"

"They make me feel like a genius."

"Sometimes truth is funny, even if it's tragic."

FAQ: What inspired you to do this?

Waiting for science experiments to run their courses is, at times, tedious. In the gaps, Wendy learned how to make a website from a Stanford sysadmin, back when the WWW was first invented. The Internet was young then and changing quickly. The excitement of learning how to shape this new media was the driving force behind her first website, which originally included a section called "Pet Porn" that showed innocent gag pictures of family pets: a kitten sleeping with a sexy negligee, the dog accidentally French-kissing Papa. Soon the annoyed sysadmin complained that Wendy's Pet Porn pages were the top-visited destination on his Stanford server. Ewww! Creeped out, she pulled down the pet pictures. The Darwin Awards stories were the second-most popular, and Wendy jibes, "My future could have gone either way."

Ancillary FAQ: What are your aspirations?

Wendy aspires to make the world a shinier place.

Wendy plans to publish a graphic novel drawn by favorite comic book artists!

Wendy yearns to become a science writer astute enough to write a book as elegant as Carl Sagan's classic, *The Dragons of Eden*.

Wendy hopes her children's book—*True Adventures of Rock, Paper, and Scissors,* squirrels raised from babies to live in the wild—will soon find a publisher.

Wendy dreams of being a science advisor for *MythBusters*. (See *MythBusters* challenge, p. 184).

FAQ: How many stories? How many books? How many more?

In your hands you hold the sixth book.

In April 2010, there were 842* stories on the website. Seven hundred have been published in six books in twenty-three languages. The Darwin Awards will live until the supply ends! Or until Wendy wins a Darwin Award while executing her latest ~~mad plan~~ innovative idea.

FAQ: Are you making a movie, musical, or TV show?

Darwin Awards: The Movie stars Joseph Fiennes and Winona Ryder, with guest appearances by *MythBusters* hosts Jamie and Adam, and the rock band Metallica. This movie is seriously silly fun. It was written and directed by Finn Taylor and filmed in the San Francisco Bay Area using plenty of stellar local talent. Check it out on DVD!

Darwin Awards: The Musical is a sensational stage play composed by Stephen Witkin, Joey Miller, and Mitch Magonet and is coming to a theatrical stage near you. When Stephen told me he wanted to write a musical, I reached for the Q-tips. A musical?! But his ideas and script are awesome. *Beach Blanket Babylon* meets *Avenue Q.* Great songs have been composed, and the show continues to be developed while seeking Off-Broadway producers.

FAQ: Do you drive while using a cell phone?

NO! And you shouldn't either.

---

* Note the beauty of this number.

Cell phones take too much attention away from the input you *ought* to attend to. Humans are not equipped to use these devices safely even while walking down the street, or piloting a shopping cart. A person on a cell phone does not notice the needs of others. In the supermarket you will not realize that you are causing aisle congestion. In a car you will drive slower and more erratically. It is very risky to drive "under the influence" of a phone.

We here at Darwin Central have made personal life changes due to reading thousands of Darwin-dumb submissions. The hardest change was to stay off our cell phones while driving. Try putting that deadly device in the backseat. Whatever it takes, get off the phone!

The life you save may be your own.

What were those Five (5) Rules, again?

Remember: To win a Darwin Award, an adult must eliminate himself from the gene pool in an astonishingly stupid way that is verifiably true.

1. Death.
2. Excellence.
3. Self-selection.
4. Maturity.
5. Veracity.

APPENDIX A

SURVIVAL TIPS

Lessons learned from the stories in this book:

Do not dunk your food into lab chemicals, however zesty.

Do not walk into a lion's cage during feeding time.

Do not swim in crocodile-infested waters.

Do not leap aboard a wild stag.

Do not lick an electrical cord that has fallen into cake batter.

Do not warm your buns inside a shrink-wrap oven.

Do not head-butt a coconut to prove a point.

Do not exit a fast-moving vehicle to prove that walking is faster.

Do not exit a fast-moving vehicle to prove that street-skating is safe.

Do not drive with a lit cigarette and a lap full of firecrackers.

Do not toss dynamite through the floorboards of your car.

Do not warm a can of paint in the oven.

Do not warm a can of lighter fuel on the stove.

Do not stick your head inside a microwave oven.

Do not leap from iceberg to iceberg, even if you can.

Do not do pull-ups on gigantic ski-lift wheels.

Do not demolish a building's supports while standing beneath it.

Do not allow yourself to be lowered into raw sewage.

Do not fix electronics while sitting on a metal toilet.

Do not muffle an explosion between your thighs.

Do not encourage a fish to swim up your urethra.

Do not romance a bench.

Do not romance a flower vase.

Do not romance a metal pipe, a raccoon, or a toilet fixture.

Do not surf on a foam air mattress.

Do not chase a feather off a cliff.

Do not steal a plane and take it on a drunken joyride.

Do not attempt to stop a train by standing in front of it.

Do not sleep in a path used by military vehicles.

Do not attach a parachute to your body and toss it out the sunroof.

Do not become mesmerized by the lyrics on your car's radio.

Do not pay back a friend by blowing up his car.

Do not dispose of suspicious dynamite by shooting it.

Do not anchor your boat with an antique bomb.

Do not fill your air mattress with flammable gas, particularly while smoking.

Do not destroy a wasp's nest with gasoline and a match.

Do not fiddle with electric wires while standing in a Jacuzzi.

Do not fiddle with electric wires while standing in a bathtub.

Do not fiddle with electric wires while standing in the rain.

Do not urinate on high voltage electrical wires, or wasp nests, or both.

Do not rappel from an electrical tower.

Do not stick the hose of an air compressor in your anus.

Do not drill into a can of paint.

Do not treat a snakebite with a Taser.

Do not load a washing machine with firecrackers.

Do not shoot yourself, even with a soft putty bullet.

Do not disguise yourself with metallic spray paint.

Do not take your kite board surfing in a hurricane.

Do not slide down a one-thousand-foot cliff face.

Do not slide down a glacier.

Do not stand directly in the path of a falling tree.

Do not examine the workings of an active tennis ball machine.

Do not leap into a large dust devil whirlwind.

Do not regard helium balloons as a mode of transportation.

Do not toss paint cans into a fire.

Do not toss propane cylinders into a fire.

Be wary of driving a motorized bar stool while drunk.

Be wary of protecting your car with a homemade electric fence.

Be wary of proving to your peers that your homemade bomb is safe.

Be wary of digging a deep tunnel beneath your house.

Be wary of digging a deep hole in wet sand.

Be wary of leaping over a sharp, pointy fence.

Be wary of wrapping yourself in plastic to lose weight.

Be wary of baking liquor-flavored cakes at a high temperature.

Be wary of overestimating the amount of explosives you need.

Be wary of pouring liquid oxygen on a fire.

Be wary of shooting soda cans from a homemade cannon.

Be wary of celebrating Independence Day with a homemade cannon.

Be wary of celebrating Independence Day with a washer full of firecrackers.

Staging a car accident is no way to obtain prescription drugs.

Staging a car accident is no way to get your insurance policy to pay up.

Staging a lion attack is no way to avoid the Draft.

It is not necessarily fun to seal yourself in a train station locker.

And always, always look before you leak.

APPENDIX B

Staff Biographies

Wendy Northcutt is the klutz behind the Darwin Awards. Wendy is a scientist and graduate of UC Berkeley with a degree in molecular biology. She began writing the Darwin Awards in 1993 and is the founder of www.DarwinAwards.com. She is the author of five previous Darwin Awards collections, and has also written and edited dozens of medical science essays. Wendy chases eclipses, hoop dances, reads comic books, enjoys natural dyes and silkwork, and pets cats whenever she can.

Kevin Buckley (kevinbuckleystudios.com) is a freelance writer/illustrator who has worked for such companies as TimeGate Studios and Pulsar Games Inc., and was a top-ten finalist in Platinum Studio's Comic Book Challenge 2007 for his comic, *The Strange and Many Eyes of Dr. LeFaux*. He has a master's degree  in Illustration from the Academy of Art University in San Francisco, where he continues to live and work alongside his ever-faithful cat, Max.

Ariane La Gauche is Wendy Northcutt's right-hand (or left-hand?) woman. She discovered the Darwin Awards as a UC Berkeley undergrad, when she spent long hours reading humorous stories online as a way of avoiding homework. Little did she know she would someday be working behind the scenes! Now based at Darwin Headquarters, Ariane corresponds with fans, does the odd bit of story editing, and feeds people. She has also sprinkled numerous enchanting turns of phrase like pixie dust on these pages. She is also a graduate student in literature. If you ask nicely, Ariane might translate the Darwin Awards into Latin. Really!

www.DarwinAwards.com/contact/ariane

Robert Adler (author of "Sex on the Brain") is a freelance science and technology writer who divides his time between Santa Rosa, California, and Oaxaca, Mexico. With a lifelong interest in science, an undergraduate degree in physics and mathematics, a PhD in psychology, and many years as a clinical and neuropsychologist, he's been lucky enough to have the opportunity to write about a surprising range of topics, from the Big Bang and black holes to multiple personalities and how to predict failed states. He's the author of hundreds of science and technology news and feature stories plus three books, most recently *Medical Firsts: From Hippocrates to the Human Genome* (Wiley, 2004). He's thrilled to appear in the Darwin Awards as the still-living author of an essay, rather than— as his wife continues to predict—the honored but unfortunately deceased recipient of a Darwin Award.

Cassandra Brooks (author of "Batty Behavior") grew up in the woods of New England, perpetually doing ecological experiments.

She loved collecting little critters from the rivers, ponds, and tide pools, investigating under what conditions they lived or died (sorry, little water striders). She was equally fond of writing it all down in her journal and sharing with her sisters and friends. After completing a Master's in marine science, studying Antarctic toothfish— one of two species better known as "Chilean Sea Bass" ("Don't eat it!")—she went back to school for science writing, finally finding a way to merge science and outreach. Her essay, while outside her field of study, is a window into a topic she's long found fascinating. "Really, don't we all?"

Alice Cascorbi (author of "Why Bother with Sex?") is a 1995 graduate of the UCSC graduate program in science writing. Her mostly academic interest in the evolution of sex was sparked by her 1988 BA thesis on that topic at Carleton College. After college, she spent several years exploring a variety of jobs in the life sciences—from sequencing oat DNA, to working as a veterinary assistant, to burning prairies for The Nature Conservancy. As of this spring, she is "all but revision" on an MS in Conservation Biology from the University of Minnesota. Before going freelance, she worked for five years at the Monterey Bay Aquarium, writing about conservation for their website and researching sustainable seafood for the Seafood Watch Program. Ecology and cooking have been two of her chief interests throughout life. When she is not writing, she enjoys mushroom hunting and organic gardening. She lives in Portland, Oregon, with her beloved husband and two Maine Coon cats.

Alison Davis (author of "RNAi: Interference by Mother Nature") is a proud banana slug alumna of the University of California,

Santa Cruz Science Communication program. She has a PhD in pharmacology from Georgetown University and did postdoctoral research in developmental biology at Stanford. A lover of science and words, Alison feeds her passions for both as a freelance writer covering Washington, D.C., where science and policy intrigue are in abundant supply. She lives near Baltimore with six males: one husband, two sons, two Australian cattle dogs, and a guinea pig.

Jennie Dusheck (author of "The Reproductive Lottery") is a freelance science writer and author of an award-winning college-level general biology textbook, with degrees in ecology and zoology. She lives in Santa Cruz, California, with her family. "My two teenage sons are big fans." Her past research life includes pursuits as disparate as analyzing the diets of free-range dairy cattle (by looking at the stomach contents of cows) to writing the protocol for a NASA Space Shuttle experiment that sent frog embryos into space. Now living on semirural property, she spends a lot of time thinking about drainage. Her essay, which could not be included in this book due to space limitation, can be found at www. DarwinAwards.com/science/lottery.html

After receiving an astrophysics degree, *Adam Mann* (author of "Quorum Sensing: Secret Language of Bacteria") joined the science writing program at UC Santa Cruz. He finds that contemplating both the cosmos and bacterial life on earth provides the same feeling: personal insignificance. He enjoys music, language, technology, and fine cheeses.

Jane Palmer (author of "Rapid Evolution") is a transplant from England who has a doctorate in computational molecular biology and a passion for climbing rocks. She lives in Boulder, Colorado, with her Scottish husband, Gareth, and her American daughter, Iona. They spend endless hours arguing over who belongs to the superior race. Iona always wins despite her small skull.

Stephanie Pappas (author of "Left Behind: Vestigial Structures") is a freelance science writer. She has a degree in psychology from the University of South Carolina and a certificate in science communication from the University of California, Santa Cruz, both institutions known for their dignified mascots (a chicken and a slug, respectively). Her favorite subjects to write about are brains, cephalopods, mummies, and medicine; one day, she'll write an article about the medical implications of a mummified cephalopod brain and retire happy. Stephanie lives in Houston, Texas, with her husband and two *very demanding* guinea pigs.

Kristin Sainani (author of "DNA Fossils: The Evolution of HIV") is a freelance science writer and a health columnist for *Allure* magazine. She is also a clinical assistant professor at Stanford University, where she teaches doctors how to write clearly and use statistics wisely. She enjoys long-distance running and hanging out with her husband and toddler.

Chandra Shekhar (author of "Evolving Cancer") turned to a career in writing after more than a decade as a scientist, and later as an entrepreneur. Although he is trained in computer science and engineering, Chandra ends up writing mostly about the life sciences. He enjoys reading Somerset Maugham, P. G. Wodehouse, Jane Austen, and other British writers, and fantasizes about writing a best-selling novel.

Mike Wall (author of "The Mystery of Super-toxic Snake Venoms") has been both a science writer and a scientist, with research interests in snake and lizard evolution and the conservation of reptiles and amphibians. He has chased down, grabbed, and been bitten by many squirmy, scaly creatures—but nothing nearly as scary as a mamba.

The Darwin Awards website was born on a Stanford University webserver in 1994. Its cynical view of the human species made it a favorite speaker in classrooms, offices, and pubs around the world. The website won dozens of Internet awards, and now ranks among the top ten thousand most-visited websites. It currently entertains a million visitors per month in its comfortable Santa Cruz home. The Darwin Awards hosts a community of free thinkers who enjoy philosophical, political, and scientific conversations. Guests are welcome to launch fireworks, bounce on the trampoline, and spin a flaming hula hoop.

Story Index

LOCATION INDEX

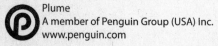